'Apologies, Good Friends...'

Our apologies, good friends, for the fracture of good order, the burning of paper instead of children, the angering of the orderlies in the front parlor of the charnel house. We could not, so help us God, do otherwise.—Daniel Berrigan

From the preface to *Night Flight to Hanoi* announcing intent to burn draft records at Catonsville, Maryland with homemade napalm.

'Apologies, Good Friends...'

AN INTERIM BIOGRAPHY OF
DANIEL BERRIGAN, S.J.

John Deedy

Fides/Claretian

Printed in the United States of America

ISBN 0-8190-0641-6

Cover design: Glenn Heinlein

Cover art: Ray Evenhouse

LC 80-28338

First printing, February 1981

Fides/Claretian

221 West Madison Street • Chicago, Illinois 60606

Contents

FOR
DAN AND EDWARD HERR,
WHO HAVE ALSO MADE A DIFFERENCE

Foreword

The scene entitled "The Spirit of 76" has been used to capture the emergence of the new nation born in the revolution. There was the resolute man in the center, beating the march of a triumphant emergence. The one on the viewing right bore proudly the bandage of suffering as he played the fife. The youngster on the left, viewing with adoration the elder, attempted to accompany the elder's beat.

The scene could be used to identify the Catholic Church as it emerged from World War II. The elders walked with heads erect for the ghost of former years had been laid to rest. The old question was answered of where American Catholics would be, and on whose side they would be, if the United States was ever at war with Italy, the home of that man who is called pope. The honor of our patriotism was unsullied by our actions. Head erect. The immigrant church had ended. We were now mainstream. We were no longer a foreign group.

The fighting men of Army, Navy, and later the Air Force proudly wore the symbol, if you remember, called the "ruptured duck." But they had been bruised in the years of absence from home and wished only to settle into the peace of that home and family.

No longer did the poverty of the depression hover over the heads of this new work force. There were jobs. The pay was good. These men turned to the officialdom of the church and asked for schools in order that their children would have the best of all that life could provide.

The church responded with a mighty building program. Education was the top priority. Our religious teachers were sent to specialize in every department of education. Alas, the one that was neglected and the last to be considered was the science of catechetics, the only reason for the building program in the first place.

John Tracy Ellis has always said that our weakest science is history. We as a nation do not know our own history, nor do we as Catholics understand our Catholic heritage. We are doomed, therefore, to repeat our mistakes.

The church in the United States became the success story. Each year the Catholic Directory illustrated the increase in membership, increase in religious vocations, increase in seminarians. There were no needs. In fact, it was widely quoted that the structure and financial affairs were second only to General Motors in efficiency.

The internal discipline was finely honed so that this growing organization which was building more and more, enlarging all of those good agencies, could serve more and more people. We were all marching to the beat of the drummer, who proud and erect was bringing us into the mainstream. What Cardinal O'Connell wished was fulfilled in Cardinal Spellman.

It was in the late '40s that the Archbishop of Boston, in speaking to the annual convention of the CYO, could say that not one bishop in the United States had a father who had a college education. It was the boast of a working-man's son who became successful as only a workingman could hope for his son. But it marked the difference between the immigrant church and the mainstream church.

Since the internal discipline was so necessary for the efficiency of this church, like unto General Motors, there was careful scrutiny of those who would be called to head the various departments, called dioceses in the canonical terms. It was necessary that loyalty to the Holy See be manifest. Who better than the friend of the Holy See to choose the department heads? It became increasingly evident that a similarity of outlook was apparent in the actions of the leaders. A blandness settled upon the church.

The transition from Pope Pius XII to the reign of Pope John XXIII was as different as the stately presence of the former to the smiling peasant appearance of the latter. So when the announcement of the need for change came and windows were opened, it had no reference to this church, now mainstream, always growing, building, and on the march. In fact, change was not possible if it upset the ongoing building of what we called the reign of God. The Council was for some other people.

There were troubling areas, but we suppressed them under the duty of citizenship. Citizenship taught us to be uncritical of the data of the moment even though those data were leading us into war. In fact war was becoming commonplace to our society which we did identify as the reign of God. Were not our wars, His wars? There was a growing struggle over civil rights which should have been called "human rights." This church of ours, successful and on the move, was not providing the leadership in stimulating the recognition of our brothers and sisters. It was busy with its own business, like the priest in the Samaritan story.

Abraham J. Heschel has a very interesting book entitled *The Prophets,* in which he studies these men, their actions, their relationship to God. He tells us: "The Prophet's eye is directed to the contemporary scene; the society and its conduct are the main theme of his speeches. Yet, his ear is inclined to God. He is a person struck by the glory and presence of God, overpowered by the hand of God. Yet his true greatness is his ability to hold God and man in a single thought."

A prophet did appear on our scene. He was a poet who seemed at the earliest moment "to hold God and man in a single thought." This is a frightening experience because it always shatters the calmed experience of the machine. It seems that we are always aware of the appearance of such a person. We seem to understand that the smoothly meshed gears of efficiency will not run again with the same evenness. That person who walked onto the scene of the American Catholic Church was Daniel J. Berrigan, S.J.

This new book written by Jack Deedy brings us into the whole life of Dan Berrigan, his family and his background. In ways intimate and revealing, the growth of the six brothers, even the division into the senior three and the junior three, illustrate the process of maturing in a very lively family.

The interplay between Dan and Phil, the mutual support of a brotherly love, has meaning for all who read. There is a serious deficiency in our communities which have not learned the lessons of love and support these brothers exemplify.

No better example of the prophet threatening the smoothly meshed gears was the powerful reaction of Cardinal Spellman to Dan Berrigan who had identified with the young man who immolated himself at the United Nations in the cause of peace. The drum, whose beat Dan Berrigan heard, clashed with the cultural patriotism which was the morality of the moment. A privatized act must be judged in the severity of its objective norm. If this act were looked upon as a call to conscience, then the whole house would collapse.

Power and oppression would be the instrument to silence the emergence of a different beat. Exile, an instrument as old as man's inhumanity, was imposed upon the prophet Dan Berrigan. It was an off-repeated expression: "Away with you."

The drumbeat of the Holy Spirit was beginning to be heard in other quarters. The figure of Dorothy Day was being evaluated anew, not in relation just to poverty, but in relation to peace and to the responsibility of the state in these matters. Dr. Martin Luther King, Jr. emerged in the leadership of the human rights issue and also the peace issue. Thomas Merton, from the Cisterian hermitage, became another voice who heard the beat of the drum of the Holy Spirit. Dan Berrigan was not alone in hearing the Word of God or, in the words of Heschel, "to hold God and man in a single thought."

It was said of Dan Berrigan, that he was a man of wrath, he was angry, and this anger revealed a deficiency in him. But it was also said of Jeremiah that he was a "prophet of wrath." It is more truly said of Dan Berrigan that, rather than being a man of wrath, he walked in an age and culture of wrath. He exposed the wrath that is hidden under the title of National Security as Martin Luther King, Jr. did in our relationship with our black brothers and sisters.

As Heschel said about the prophet, "he is a person who knows what time it is," so Berrigan knew that the hour had struck and the value of the gospel was the beat of the drummer, the Spirit of God. He was walking through the streets of America, a new precursor, crying out, "make straight the paths."

Jack Deedy has enriched us with his book, *"Apologies, Good Friends. . ."*

†CARROLL T. DOZIER
Memphis, Tennessee

Introduction

Ted Morgan said it at lunch in a restaurant in Boston's North End a few days after his Somerset Maugham biography was published: "You don't write biographies about living people—you don't even write biographies about people who have just died. There's a time element needed for the individual to fall into perspective."

In the context of those remarks, this book about Father Daniel Berrigan, S.J., may seem chronologically out of place, an act of presumption. Except, this book is not intended as biography in the formal sense. At best it is an interim biography of a person who is not only not dead, but alive and very much evolving still. Dan Berrigan is quite literally a pilgrim, a journeyer with a mission. Whatever one might think of his style or his manner of doing things, Berrigan has a fascinating historical past. He stands on the threshold of his 60th year as this book is written, and it is safe to predict that his seventh decade will be as interesting, perhaps as wondrous as earlier ones. I write this, for instance, on a cold, late August Wednesday in 1980; next Sunday, Berrigan flies to Ireland with two of his brothers to fast and pray on behalf of political prisoners being held in H Block at Long Kesh in Northern Ireland. He doesn't have to go. It would be more convenient to stay in New York City or even to go down to Washington and demonstrate once again outside the Pentagon. He flies to Ireland because people there are suffering—political prisoners. He identifies with sufferers and does not need a whole lot of encouragement to put himself out on their behalf. The Ireland visit could set a pattern for the 1980s, but then again the Ireland visit is a part of the pattern of the past.

By any measurement, Dan Berrigan is a colorful figure, and colorful figures are the stuff of books. More pertinently, and without making him seem impossibly holy or stuffily apostolic, Berrigan is a motivated person, and as such becomes a natural subject for a book in the series being planned by Fides/Claretian on individuals who have taken a lead in confronting current social problems. The purpose of this series is not to transform readers of the books into fierce radicals or types of apostolic "nuts." It is simply to dramatize a little of what is possible when motivation exists. Berrigan once wrote in *U.S. Catholic:* "Even with the most fervent will, it is not possible for everyone to do everything. We cannot level our lance at every evil, right every wrong. But we can do something, and the moral distance between doing something and doing nothing is momentous indeed." If people reading this or another book in the Fides/Claretian series feel moved to make a personal and spiritual commitment to a cause, fine. If these books just raise the awareness of people a little to a problem, to an injustice, to a course of corrective action, well that's fine too.

It is not the purpose of this book to whip up a cadre of latter-day draft-board raiders, or even to mobilize people for a militant confrontation of the arms race. This book is not intended as a polemic. However, if some feel moved by the "people examples" offered to make a change in their lives, incrementally, without completely uprooting themselves, without turning into barn burners, then at least one author in the series will not be disappointed.

Which is to say that I am perhaps not the best person in

the world to be writing this book. I do not approach it with an ideological or a personal detachment. I admire Dan Berrigan as an individual, and over the years I have shared his concerns about war and peace, the Bomb and the survival of humanity. When the chips were on the table in a big way, however, during the Vietnam war, I took the safer, easier course. While Berrigan and others went the activist route, I went to the typewriter. Over those bitter years, my writings were of sufficient ideological correctness for me to win approval of many in the Catholic left. So it was that the very first article which Berrigan wrote from the underground, when he was on the run from the FBI, was posted to me. I was managing editor of *Commonweal* at the time, and the piece appeared in the magazine's issue of May 29, 1970 under the title "Notes from the Underground; or I Was a Fugitive from the FBI." I prize to this day the note accompanying the manuscript. Warm and friendly, it asked me to "please forget the postmark on the envelope." "Not anxious to help the opposition," Dan added. I was so conscientious about the request, and so paranoid about FBI "gumshoes," that I wasted not a second in tearing the envelope into the tiniest pieces. I couldn't resist peeking at the postmark, however. It was stamped in Boston. I must say, my paranoia was not entirely misplaced. FBI agents dropped around *Commonweal* in their hunt for Berrigan. I also suspect that my home telephone came under surveillance after an article of mine on Berrigan, still on the run, appeared in the *New York Times*. But I am not absolutely certain of that. If there is an FBI file on me, it might show in that record, but I was never interested enough to check it out.

All this sounds dramatic and somewhat meaningful now, but it really wasn't significant in any historical sense.

My witness was miles short of Berrigan's and others in the American Catholic left, and I felt it. I forever had a conscience, for instance, about taking the late-night train home from Grand Central to secure, detached Larchmont, after attending a peace meeting or rally in New York City. It was especially bad the night Phil Berrigan was corralled in the rectory of St. Gregory the Great church up on 90th Street. Usually my guilt feelings would have begun to subside by the time the train got out around New Rochelle. Not that night.

Looking back, the principal consolation of those years is that I was the conduit out of jail for two Berrigan-type activists. One was by helping manufacture a job at *Commonweal* for Jim Forest, one of the Milwaukee 14. It was a short-term job. He needed it in order to qualify for parole. For the other—Tom Lewis—it was signing some kind of paper of stewardship or guardianship, a paper guaranteeing one thing or another—that he intended to "go straight," that I felt he belonged back in society, that I'd help get him to court. My mind is foggy on the specifics. I merely know that if my responsibility was to be a Dutch uncle of sorts, a surrogate on behalf of prudence or of law and order, I wasn't much help to authorities. My "charge" went on from blood-pouring in Baltimore to incineration of draft records at Catonsville.

In 1971, after the Camden 28 action, I held a defense-fund party at my house in Larchmont for John Peter Grady, a prime mover in that action group. The party attracted people in cars taking notes and license-plate numbers, and a flock of close friends. But this was not witness. This was lark. The party went on to the very wee hours, turning a bit boozy and boisterous in the process. It was a terrific social success, and a small financial one too, as I recall. I had too good a time to know exactly, or to be able to claim to have done anything real for the movement—unless it was to shake up Larchmont a bit. Larchmont needed shaking up.

What I am saying, I guess, is that as one who dallied on the fringe of the peace movement, I feel a debt to those who went the full distance in the cause of peace. I feel a special debt to Dan Berrigan. I should, therefore, perhaps turn this writing task over to someone who was above it all and who could accordingly be dispassionate. But that would mean finding someone who had been hermetically sealed off from trends and events for ten years or so. Or it would mean awaiting the coming to writing age of the then-baby generation. The former is impossible; the Fides/Claretian deadline does not allow the latter. So I proceed.

I do not serve up here the definitive Dan Berrigan book. I have seized upon the principal details of his life—his growing up, his education, certain of his 41 years as a Jesuit—to convey some idea of where he came from, where he goes, and by what motivation. In researching the book, I have talked to scores of people and traveled to a half-score or more cities: New York City, a couple of times; Baltimore, Ithaca, Syracuse, even Manchester-by-the-Sea, Massachusetts. The person lives there who proposed Berrigan for the Melcher Book Award, given by the Unitarian Universalist Association each year for the most significant contribution to religious liberalism. The award to Berrigan was presented in 1971 for three books published in 1970: *No Bars to Manhood, The Trial of the Catonsville Nine,* and *Trial Poems* (illustrations by Thomas Lewis). Berrigan was behind bars at the time, and Unitarian-Universalist officials wrote to the warden asking permission for Berrigan to attend the award banquet in Washington, D.C. The warden said no.

Some of my most fascinating research for this book was carried out in the Department of Rare Books at Cornell University Library. The Berrigan papers are located there, alongside other prized collections: the George Bernard Shaw collection, one of the three best Shaw collections in the world; the Dante and Petrarch collections, perhaps the best in the Western hemisphere; the papers of General Lafayette; records of the abolitionist movement. It is good company to be in. The Berrigan collection is mountainous. As of January 17, 1980 there was a total of 58,323 items in the collection: manuscripts, letters, newspaper clippings, arrest notices, trial files, and miscellany. Three more large cartons were as yet uncataloged. In my research, I did not begin to dent the collection. However, I did read through files that I considered important in the writing of this book, such as the file of letters from Thomas Merton, the Trappist. It was an exciting experience.

I owe gratitude to so many persons for assistance in the preparation of this book that it is dangerous to list anyone. But I must express thanks to the Berrigan family in Baltimore and in Syracuse for its cooperation, and to Jim Tyler, the curator "in effect" of the Berrigan papers at Cornell. (Incidentally, that collection includes the papers of Philip Berrigan and Elizabeth McAlister, as well.) I must also cite Francine du Plessix Gray, whose essay on the Berrigan brothers in her book *Divine Disobedience* is invaluable to a researcher into Berrigan history. She makes the writer's work easier, but at the same time more difficult; she is that thorough and perceptive on the Berrigans, she does not leave much unexplored territory. I should thank the staff of the Carnegie Library in Rockport for services over and above the call of duty in turning up Berrigan books and material from throughout the Eastern Massachusetts library system. And I should thank Dan Berrigan himself for his availability for taping sessions in New York City, and most particularly for laying out so much of the vital record beforehand in his books of prose and of poetry. They amount to a veritable autobiography, though inevitably a strung-out one. His books number to thirty, and counting. His life, his thought is on every page of them. Some of the Berrigan quotes in this book are from his books of conversation; more are from fresh tapes made with me at his apartment in New York City.

Finally, I should acknowledge Mary Ann and Mace Wenniger, whose graphic-arts gallery in Rockport provided some necessary ambience in the writing of this book—or at least in its researching. I spell my wife at their gallery late afternoons and evenings, and many's the Berrigan book that was read between allocutions on the difference between a collagraph and an etching. Many's the eye too that boggled at seeing Berrigan books sitting around an art gallery in proper, very proper, arty Rockport.

My look at Berrigan will be different I trust, from that which other writers have taken. It focuses attention on the Catholic dimension, for it is obvious that Catholicism is embedded in the man and impels him in unique ways. This is not merely a born Catholic. This is no perfunctory Catholic, no Catholic by accident or in name only. Daniel Berrigan is often compared to an Old Testament prophet, a Jeremiah going about crying out against a doomsday folly. Indeed, there is much of the Old Testament prophet in him. There's a touch of the Buddhist in him too, for that matter. But essentially Dan Berrigan is a New Testament Christian, a Gospel-oriented, baptized, believing, practicing Catholic. He is not, however, your standard-brand parish Catholic. He's anything but that. That's the glory of his life. He'd say it's his salvation.

J.D.
Rockport, Ma., 1980

1

Coming of Age, Gradually

—1—

It is not a monk's cell, but it is perhaps as close as a person could come to finding one in throbbing, unmonkish Manhattan Island. This "cell" is an apartment, actually—11 stories above Broadway in the west 90s, the Upper West Side in the parlance of New Yorkers. The apartment is spacious by Manhattan standards: four rooms and hallway. There are high ceilings, windows to the north, lots of wall space. These walls, including those of kitchen and bathroom, are a festival of wit and art and nostalgia. The apartment's furnishings, on the other hand, are meager. No grand rugs on the floor. A single, twin-sized bed without headboard, a desk and a chair in one room. A compact, stand-up kitchen. A dated bathroom. A living room with small circular table, four plastic-mold chairs, a bookcase. There is no easy chair, no divan ensemble. The television set sits ignominiously on the floor, its front end propped with books for viewing angle; it is turned on for the news, little else. The apartment is neat; it is plain; it throbs with life. A veritable forest of plants competes for sun and light. Over against one wall in the living room is a mound of pillows, clue that people come here in number. The gatherings are frequent, in fact, and these are the seats of comfort.

This is Daniel Berrigan's apartment, and Dan Berrigan, Catholic priest, Jesuit in good standing, attracts people as a magnet attracts metal—not all people, as Berrigan is not everyone's magnetic force, but many people, or some as the times may dictate. They would be people concerned as he is about justice and rights and the survival in dignity of that which is graciously called humankind. We may be sinless people, in our own eyes, says Berrigan, but we are also victims whose fate it may well be to witness the end of the world, to be part of that end, its passive tinder and fuel. He fears the world is headed for nuclear holocaust. He works for disarmament.

The Berrigan apartment is clue to the person and psyche of its occupant. Next to the popes, and not discounting a media eclipse of the past several years— an eclipse which even popes have been known to experience—Dan Berrigan for two decades has been one of the most publicized priests in Christendom. Yet there are no scrapbooks about this apartment, no file of clippings of the praise and detraction, no record of the triumphs and setbacks that have been his. *Time* magazine once put him on its cover; authors, reporters, editorialists have written reams about him. There's no hint of this, or very little. His own written books count to thirty, but the volumes in his bookcase are books of meditation, books by Thoreau, Melville, Gandhi. Honors have been his, but the plaques, scrolls, medals are elsewhere. There is, however, a copy of his arrest record from the files of the New York City Police Department, complete with fingerprints. The arrest and disposition spaces are filled, confirmation of course to Dan Berrigan that as a man of conscience he is living his moral convictions. This indeed may be his proudest possession.

On the bedroom wall there is that famous picture of Dan Berrigan and his brother Philip, a Josephite priest who subsequently married, torching draft records rifled from

Local Board No. 33 in Catonsville, Maryland one May day in 1968. But only the carper would seize upon the presence of that picture as a symbol of vanity. The picture records a pivotal moment in Dan Berrigan's career as a Jesuit and as an American. Pivotal moments are for remembering and renewing.

Most of the pictures are of family and friends: his parents; the six Berrigan brothers; nieces, nephews; the great-uncle who moved from ploughboy to priest; the aunt, Sister Maria Josephine of the Sisters of Charity of Mount St. Vincent, who became something of a legend in her order for her work among the immigrant folk and among the people in Harlem; Dorothy Day, a special hero; Rose Hawthorne Lathrop, daughter of Nathaniel Hawthorne, Catholic convert and founder of the Dominican Sisters of the Congregation of St. Rose of Lima. Why Rose Hawthorne Lathrop? The connection is with a cancer hospital for the indigent on Jackson Street on New York's lower east side. This is St. Rose's Free Home for Incurable Cancer—94 beds, 336 patients over a year's time. Rose Hawthorne Lathrop's order runs that hospital, and Dan Berrigan helps out there, usually on Thursdays, 10 a.m. to 4 p.m. He is there not as chaplain. The Capuchin Fathers of Stanton Street handle that assignment. Berrigan is there "just to be there," to make friends with patients and their families, to hold the very sick, to help feed the feeble, to wheel about the invalid, to run errands. He's a kind of orderly-at-large. "When people are that close to death, they become very childlike. They love sweets, and it's a great thing to get a milk shake for them. Or coffee. I take orders for them." Dan Berrigan speaks modestly, almost reluctantly of this volunteer work. It has been going on for more than three years. He also borrows time from himself

to go to the Bronx to teach a course in "black prison literature" at a "poor people's college" called New Resources.

The work in the cancer ward is especially important to
Berrigan. "I find it necessary to have some physical work
connected with suffering," he explains. "It is self-testing. It
is an exploration of one's response to death by cancer,
which now appears to be, in the world of the Bomb, the
declared vocation of humanity. Experiencing cancer is a
rehearsal for the future as presently planned. Being with
those dying of cancer is to be with those among whom the
Bomb has already fallen, and this is a privilege. Those we
care for, the experience of their sufferings, helps me find
my way to the Pentagon and the White House and the
places where our communities join in resistance to a future
of death and cancer."

Finally, there is on the wall of Berrigan's apartment a
crucifix, but not your standard crucifix. This one is made
from barbed wire snipped from a fence around a Trident
submarine base. The Trident is the latest in underwater
nuclear sophistication. It spells evil for Berrigan,
epitomizes everything that is sinister about the nation's
emphases: armaments before people, guns before butter,
Baal before Christ. The "Trident crucifix" speaks to Berrigan as no Barclay Street crucifix could. Visual heresies,
Berrigan calls those Barclay Street, mass-produced
crucifixes with their often garish, overly humanized, artis-
tically insipid images of the Savior undergoing death. His
"Trident crucifix" is stark, as piercing to the eye as to the
touching finger. It has no representational human form,
no anatomically rendered Christ of the cross. It needs
none, and speaks to Berrigan better without one. It is
graphic reminder to Berrigan of the God whose son died
for the sins of man, and of the world which may die a

death of its own because of the folly of humankind, specifically nuclear folly.

A new generation of Americans, and some from the older generations, is preoccupied with the dangers of commercial nuclear power, and Dan Berrigan concedes that nuclear power is "one blade with two edges pressed against us." But when Berrigan is arrested nowadays, it is at the Pentagon, not at Seabrook, say, where the Public Service Company of New Hampshire doggedly presses construction of a nuclear power facility. Berrigan's explanation is simple: "The nation could decide this year, and well may decide within a few years to dump nuclear energy. It's not working. It's getting too expensive. It's too dangerous, and people are getting aroused. And a decision like that would by no means inhibit or halt or even mitigate the nuclear arms race." So Dan Berrigan has taken on the nuclear arms society.

All of this makes for a very intense individual, but anything but a dreary person. Dan Berrigan is in fact a fascinating combination of the profoundly dedicated man and the man with the wit to relax and smile, occasionally at himself. Thus on the bedroom wall is yet another picture, this one a small, faded, romanticized print of the Old Testament's Daniel facing the lions in the den. Most everyone knows the print who ever opened a pictorial bible history: brave Daniel alone, the lions withdrawn, timorous before God's witness. The print hangs in mock solemnity. "It was given to me as a joke," Berrigan laughs.

Whimsical the picture may be to Berrigan, yet it does sum up much of his life as priest and citizen. Dan Berrigan has braved the lions of church and state for decades. Before the government slapped him into federal prison for destroying draft records, religious superiors had dispatched him to Latin America in an attempt to temper his zealousness for peace, which some somehow saw as unpatriotic. Berrigan not only survived, but he returned to cry the louder about the perversions of peace and justice. Even from prison his voice came across the walls to the nation at large.

For years Dan Berrigan was a prime figure in the news, a darling of television and the press. That has changed. Today it often seems as if Dan Berrigan speaks to an empty theater. He does not draw media coverage, certainly not in terms comparable to the past. Television cameras are pointed elsewhere, and the press gives him what appears to be begrudging paragraphs. He was arrested one winter's day of 1980 for sitting-in with several others in the office of the president of the University of California in a protest against that institution's management of Lawrence Livermore and Los Alamos weapons laboratories. The media hardly noticed. For the media he seems to be yesterday's news story.

Dan Berrigan is philosophical about this and at the same time contemptuous of the media, associating them with that "tremendous network of power and monetary interest that says, 'this is the way this country is going to conduct its business in the world, and we are this country.'" What's more, he finds nothing of present media indifference unpredictable in terms of the past. "The media always came late and lazy and cowardly to the war," he remarks, alluding of course to the Vietnam period. "They followed events and never formed them, and if Nixon really barked or Johnson raised hell, the media disappeared, as we found out on so many occasions when great events would get no coverage." Berrigan is not unduly distressed over the current lack of coverage. "Others can speak for themselves," he comments, "but I have felt a kind of cold comfort in these later years that whatever we've been able to do has had to be quite serious and conscientious, because the media were not around and you didn't have that kind of media glamour in the side of your eye that might lead you to do things without deeply examining yourself and your motives and your life."

So the media have drifted off, and the ranks of partisans of his causes are thin compared to the Vietnam years. But Berrigan is serene. He has his peace community in New York. His brother Philip and Philip's wife Elizabeth McAlister, a former religious of the Sacred Heart of Mary, continue to fight the good fight with a core group in Baltimore. Resistance communities are springing up here and there. And around the country he constantly meets in his travels saving remnants, people young and some not so young, all of them anxious to work for a peace that is not a mere balance of terror, but a peace that is genuine in the biblical sense. In this context, the shunning by the media may be a blessing. "Maybe it will result in a different breed of Catholic coming along," he philosophizes, "one that will be more patient with time and won't give up so easily." Dan Berrigan, for one, has no intention of giving up.

—2—

Life's journey has taken Daniel Berrigan along controversial and sometimes exotic pathways: behind the Iron Curtain, for instance, when travel to Eastern Europe was still severely restricted—in fact, he was one of the first American priests to be granted visas to Hungary and Czechoslovakia, when the Iron Curtain began to lift; to Latin America, on what was intended as disciplinary exile, but which turned into an education in the meaning of oppression and poverty; to Hanoi, when that North Vietnamese city was under the rain of American bombs; to Underground, U.S.A. as a fugitive from the law, with virtually the entire corps of the Federal Bureau of Investigation in pursuit; to Block Island, off Rhode Island, but not for vacationing (this was Last Stop, Underground U.S.A.); to the federal penitentiary at Danbury, Connecticut as prisoner #23742-125; to the Middle East, to Alaska, to Catonsville, Maryland. Always he has traveled as a pilgrim for peace.

Life itself began inauspiciously in Virginia, Minnesota, a rural community some 50 miles above Duluth. Daniel was born May 9, 1921, the fifth of six sons of Thomas and Frida Berrigan. His mother was a Fromhart, an immigrant from Germany, who landed at Ellis Island at age five and was taken to northern Minnesota, where the Fromharts had a land claim, where they built a cabin, and where the Fromhart men pursued careers as miners and farmers. Tom Berrigan, born in Iowa of Tipperary parents, arrived in Minnesota as a railroad engineer with the Mesabi Iron Ore Company. He and Frida were married June 21, 1911, Tom's 32nd birthday, by a Croatian priest who was a missioner to the Indians, a Monsignor Joseph Buh, a man with a reputation for being a saint. A picture of Buh, in full whiskers, occupies a place of honor in Berrigan's bedroom picture gallery.

Frida and Tom Berrigan did not stay in Minnesota. Times were tough, work was seasonal and subject to the fluctuations of the economy. In addition, Tom was active in the Socialist party, a matter which did not endear him to employers. Inevitably he was in and out of work. Restless, disgruntled, feeling a stranger among the Swedes and

Norwegians who were predominant in the area, Tom persuaded Frida to pack up the family and join a colony of Irish farmers near Syracuse. His own family had gone there from Iowa, and the Minnesota Berrigans, now at their full complement—mother, father, six sons—were soon behind them, placing down roots near the town of Liverpool. The move bedevils Dan Berrigan's memory to this day, not because he would have preferred upstate Minnesota to upstate New York—geographical preferences at age five are almost nonexistent—but because the move had a kind of unilateral quality about it. Dado, the boys' name for their father, wanted to be with his family and with the Irish, and in the Berrigan family the father's will dominated. "He was never very affectionate toward my mother," Dan Berrigan reflected recently. "He kept his own clan first, and she being German was an outsider. We reacted very strongly to that, the kids did. We didn't like that."

Tom Berrigan may have been born in Iowa, but he was Irish to the stereotype: florescent in his Catholicism, after an early excursion into religious indifference; towering in his rages; certain in his knowledge of things; demanding of the family; bright, interested and concerned about matters of the mind. He was an avid writer of poetry, which he committed to memory and would lay on the family at the drop of a syllable. Tom's poetry was not published; it went into trunks. When he was not reciting his own writings, he would dip into Shakespeare, Yeats, or Francis Thompson. The content was improved but for the family not the experience. The boys listened docilely, though as a group they were physically far from docile. Most brothers fight as young boys, and the Berrigans were no exception. Indeed, fights sometimes extended upward to the father. Phil

Berrigan has told of seeing his father strangely becalmed one morning at breakfast table, his face marked by cuts and bruises. "One of your brothers and I had a good, good fight," Tom announced. There was a contentment in his tone.

The father was often a trial to the family, but love and respect flowed upward and downward. One of Dan Berrigan's most beautiful poems, certainly one of his most touching, is one written from Danbury prison in which he thanks the father for giving his children "the best of your juice and brawn."

> Whatever you denied us, you
> gave us this which enemies name
> distemper, madness; our friends,
> half in despair, arrogance.
> Which I name, denying both—the best of
> your juice and brawn—unified
> tension to good purpose.

The poem, entitled "My Father," appears in Berrigan's *Prison Poems.*

The mother, by contrast, was quiet, gentle, patient, and the move east, though perhaps taken against her better judgment, did nothing to unsettle a happy marriage. Tom worked at a number of jobs—with the diocese of Syracuse, as an engineer in one of its orphanages; with the Syracuse Lighting Company; with the WPA, as a foreman on construction projects; back with the light company, now called Niagara-Mohawk; on defense jobs during World War II. At the same time, with the help of the boys he ran a seven-acre farm. All had their designated chores—milking the cows, ploughing, planting, harvesting, canning for the winter. Gifted with his hands, the father taught the boys a number of useful trades, although some eluded Dan. He was frail growing up, so while the rugged types were outside working with the father, Dan was inside helping the mother. Hers was an example and theirs a relationship that markedly influenced his life.

Those were the Depression years, and the Berrigans felt the pinch. The *Catholic Worker* came to the house, and so did magazines like *Commonweal* and *America*. The latter came courtesy of the clan, for magazine subscriptions were a luxury in Tom Berrigan's home. The Berrigans were poor. As a farm family, however, much of their living came off the land, and the dinner table was well stocked. In fact, theirs was a bounty to be shared. "My mother was extremely hospitable, and my father too, I would say, and we always had a lot of poor people around," Dan Berrigan recalls. It was a time, of course, when thousands of men were on the road—jobless in search of work, hobos in flight from their past, or in search of a future, drifters of all sort uprooted by the Depression and turned loose on the landscape. They hitchhiked, and they walked, and they hopped rides on freight trains. The railroad passed very near the Berrigan farm, and wanderers were constantly popping in. It is claimed—although the Berrigans do not know it for sure—that there was a mark on the barn, left by one departing wanderer to let others know that here one could get a meal or a bunk. The drifters were welcome without exception, or reservation. "We had some pretty tough characters there over the years," Berrigan declares, "and much of the time my mother was alone with the smallest kids. But she was absolutely fearless." The voice rings with admiration.

When Frida Berrigan wasn't bunking the tired and feeding the hungry stranger at her kitchen table, she was sending food around the neighborhood. There was a cart on the farm, and she would load it up with milk and fruits and vegetables, and send the boys off to distribute the items among the needy. "That was very influential on us," Berrigan comments, "that we shared food and lodging, even though we didn't otherwise have a great deal ourselves." Especially meaningful to Berrigan was that the sharing did not spring from some mere humanitarian or secularist instinct. "My mother was very deeply religious in a way I could always grab," he remarks. "My mother was someone who believed very deeply, was very contemplative, and didn't talk a lot—about religion or anything else. But, sure, her motivation in sharing was very religious. You did this because this is the way you lived as a Christian."

When Dan and his brother Phil were on trial years later for torching draft records of a Selective Service office, they would cite the mother's influence of simple Christian charity as motivation for their acts.

—3—

The educational years are not years that Dan Berrigan looks back on with particular fondness, beginning with parochial school. He attended St. John the Baptist Academy in Syracuse for both grade and high school, 12 "long" years with a 13th tacked on because the Jesuits wanted a stronger Latin background in the candidate who had applied for admission to the order. At St. John the Baptist, Berrigan was at the top of his class, but that appears to have been neither triumph nor palliative. "It was horrible," he says. "The school was pre-everything." But there was no other choice. The Berrigan boys were told where to go to school, and they went. "It was not the most exciting part of any one of our lives," he comments. "In fact, we just endured; and they endured us, I'm sure," he says—the last by way of affectionate reference to nuns he respects and who, he feels, were no less hostages to the old system than he considers himself to have been. The nuns were members of the Sisters of St. Joseph.

More stimulating was the auxiliary education that Berrigan was receiving at home through books. "My father was a terrific reader, and my mother was always lugging books back and forth from the library. Everything was around the house: fiction, poetry, plays, Shakespeare. We read everything, but mainly the classics. We just never stopped reading." The father's tastes dominated reading habits, and they ran to 19th-century writers: Dickens, Thackeray, and poets such as Shelley, Wordsworth, Keats, and Tennyson. Dan Berrigan's penchant for good reading and his inclinations toward poetry can be traced back to these years. "We were distant from the movies, and we had a radio toward high school, but my father was unenthused about any of that stuff, whether it was the radio or the movies. So reading was the order of the day, really. That or work."

Dan Berrigan entered the Jesuits at age 18, reporting August 14, 1939 for two years of novitiate study at St. Andrew-on-Hudson in Poughkeepsie, 75 miles above New York City. He and a friend had investigated by mail a number of religious orders and inclined toward the Jesuits partly because the Jesuits didn't seem to want them. "All the other orders were trying to rope us in by showing us photographs of jazzy swimming pools in their prospectus," he once told author Francine du Plessix Gray. "But the 'Jebbies' just had a couple of tight little quotes from St.

Ignatius in a very stark pamphlet. We thought that cool scene was revolutionary." The truly determining influence, however, was a five-volume history of the North American martyrs that the father had about the house. Berrigan had never met a Jesuit, but the history was introduction sufficient. "Learning about the Jesuit martyrs was very important at that stage of my life," he says. The North American martyrs became the more alive to Berrigan because he lived the scene, so to speak. The Syracuse area was Mohawk territory and nearby was Auriesville, where three Jesuit missionaries were martyred by Mohawk Indians. Berrigan used to visit there.

Dan Berrigan carries a strong commitment to the Jesuit life, but no large affection for the training by which he arrived at final vows. At St. Andrew's, he says, "we were under a regime that even in Europe would seem hair-raising." His novice master was Father Leo Weber, something of a legend in the order, very complicated—charismatic, they would say now—tough, traditional. "What he put himself through to get us young characters in shape for this here life is beyond belief," Berrigan declares; and what Weber put the novices through pierces Berrigan's memory 40 years later. In addition to a rigorous life of prayer and study, there was hard physical work helping to keep going the huge piece of real estate that was St. Andrew's. The novices were the hired hands, doing everything from scrubbing and waxing floors, to cleaning toilets, washing dishes, and working on the grounds. The property has since been sold, taken over by the Culinary Institute of America for use as a cooking school and restaurant, a fate that novices of Berrigan's era would no doubt say is deserved.

"It was very military," Berrigan says of his novitiate. "In

fact, Leo Weber was constantly using military metaphors out of West Point. You see, we were right near West Point and we were supposed to comport ourselves like West Pointers. Everyone parted his hair on the same side, used his knife and fork in the same way; no one crossed his legs, let alone his ankles, and you sat up straight." Everything was monitored, one's walk, one's hair, one's speech, and anything out of line was criticized. "If you didn't like it, you were invited to leave very soon."

Summer provided no respite. The novices got a couple of weeks off for what was called villa. "Of course, you didn't leave the grounds," says Berrigan. "You now went into a rigorous program of recreation, which was more exhausting than ever. You had to be thrashing about on land, on water, or in the air. You had to be doing something every hour of the day—and in that steam pit of the Hudson River Valley. I can remember the sweat pouring off me, 'cause you were always in a cassock or these horrible prison greys—denim jacket and dark grey or black work pants. We looked like we were from San Quentin." For a nonathletic type, novitiate vacation to Berrigan was no vacation at all.

Berrigan lasted, of course, and moved to the other side of the house for juniorate. The emphasis now was on Latin, Greek, and English, and Berrigan found he had a lot of catching up to do. He had no Greek; his Latin, despite that extra high-school year of tutorial study, was "so-so." His educational background, in sum, was no where near that of the "whiz kids"—his term—from the Jesuit prep schools of the New York City and Buffalo areas. The juniorate class was divided into A and B sections. Berrigan was placed in the B group.

The intellectual challenges attracted Berrigan, notably

the public testing of his writing ability. He dispatched a poem, "Storm Song," to *America* and found himself something of a minor celebrity when it was accepted and published. "That was a great kudos, my heavens, in those days—1942," he comments. The acceptance by *America* encouraged Berrigan to write more poetry, which he enjoyed and indulged himself in prolifically. At the same time he was discovering Gerard Manley Hopkins and others of the modern writers, and this too was stimulating. But the rest of the training he found pure drudgery. "It would be considered torture now," he exclaims.

The memory stirs a sadness in Berrigan that, as one with a love of learning, he never experienced an education that was joyous or that he feels was addressed to his own talents. His learning was under a heavy hand, he says, and came as if stamped out of a forge. "But you got used to it," he remarks. "That's your AMDG, I guess." Your degree. The comment is a play on the motto of the Jesuit order, *Ad Majorem Dei Gloriam,* For the Greater Glory of God.

After Poughkeepsie, it was Woodstock, Maryland for three years of philosophy, a period that Berrigan, half-serious, half in jest, calls the "nadir of my noncareer." "I detested it," he says. "I couldn't connect with that stuff. Latin classes in logic and metaphysics. Whew. In the second year it was a little better as we had better teachers. But psychology and cosmology; oh God, dreadful. It was just sterile. Logically, it was the bare bones of the Jesuit skull, and I wasn't made that way. The prayers were in Latin. The classes were in Latin. The exams were in Latin. Life was grey—g-r-e-y—, and we grew grey before our times. I stayed the course and passed the exams but, again, it was just on that level. Everyone waited for 'salvation,' because at the end of three years you were to be liberated to go out teaching. So you hung on."

There are clues to the future Daniel Berrigan in this Berrigan of seminary years. A person of such impatience with the abstract, of such contempt for the abstruse, of such passion for directness is indeed a person who could be disposed to brush aside the niceties of language and behavior in order to drive a point home, or seek to correct a situation he conceived to be unjust. But no one should be misled by Berrigan's criticism of his Jesuit beginnings, nor by some subsequent clashes with Jesuit superiors, into believing that this is a man who would one day walk indignantly away from the Jesuit order.

However, Dan Berrigan admits to having had such impulses, and on at least two occasions his close friend Thomas Merton, the Trappist—Father M. Louis, O.C.S.O.—helped rein him in. Once was in the spring of 1963, when Berrigan, then on the faculty of Le Moyne College in Syracuse, was denied permission to take part in a freedom ride in support of civil rights of blacks. "A violent break with superiors would only tend to cast discredit on all the initiatives you have so far taken and render them *all* suspect as part of a dangerous process leading to radicalization and defection," Merton wrote in counsel. "If you allow this to happen, you must consider that you are turning adrift those who have begun to follow you and profit by your leadership, and you are also at the same time wreaking havoc in the minds of superiors who were perhaps timidly beginning to go along with you."

A second time came early in the Vietnam war period— November, 1965—after Berrigan was banished to Latin America from New York City because of peace activities that offended the patriotic propensities of Francis Cardinal Spellman and no doubt also of his own Jesuit superiors. "For one, I have never managed to get awful sorry for your going to Latin America," wrote Merton. "It is where everything is going to happen." Berrigan, in other words, could count himself lucky, and indeed the four-month exile did add dimensions of sensitivity, and indignation, to the man. It was his education in the meanings of rebellion and repression. When he returned in March of 1966, Merton welcomed him home with a note saying, "Glad things have cleared. I thought they might. Go to it, man! Maybe with this dirty war the nation will learn a few things about itself and grow up."

Berrigan thus stayed a Jesuit, and he is determined to remain one. He concedes his love for the order is "a little quirky," but at the same time he says he feels "a deep sense of belonging" in the order. Perhaps part of it is the order's revolutionary tradition. Jesuits on several continents, in several centuries have been willing to die for their beliefs; English Jesuits of the 16th and 17th centuries went underground to vindicate the unity of the church. Berrigan unquestionably sees himself in something of their tradition. "I remember my superior at *Jesuit Missions* saying once, 'The reason you're having so much trouble is that you're a Jesuit,' and I thought that wasn't bad," he remarks. He adds, "I have tried to grab the spirit of the order and run with it." He is talking of a spirit to which, he is convinced, many of today's Jesuits have become strangers.

On nonideological levels, there is in Berrigan a sense of debt to the order that received him, educated him, ordained him, an order in which he has found so many of the friends of his life. Additionally there is the feeling that "the hard times are over" and that many of the things he fought for over the years are in the air. "I picked up the national Jesuit paper the other day," he said one spring day in 1980, "and I see that five young Jesuits are in jail in the state of Washington over the Trident submarine." There was a touch of satisfaction and admiration in the voice, as if the long and often lonesome years of questioning, of protesting, of being arrested and imprisoned were suddenly worth it for the consciousness over peace, justice, and human survival quickened in a new generation of Jesuits.

Finally, there is for Berrigan the question of alternatives to life as a Jesuit. "I look around me at America," he says, "and I have to seriously ask myself, 'Where do you go?' I do not find much human excitement around."

On the other hand, what if push came to shove out of the order, as almost happened at least once in the past? At the height of his antiwar activities, a provincial flew to Rome to put a halt to an expulsion proceeding; he did this less out of regard for Berrigan—the provincial in fact was neither fan nor admirer—than out of concern for the disruption within the order that expulsion would have caused. On any possible departure from the order, Berrigan is emphatic. "They will have to kick me out and take the heat," he says. This has been his mind since he got his land legs as a Jesuit. "I am staying, because I feel myself a Jesuit."

Vow or threat, Berrigan's determination would seem to guarantee that those within the Jesuit order who do not like the Berrigan mode will have to endure their hair shirt for years to come. Berrigan turns 60 in 1981, youthful looking and generally in better health than he has been for years. If family history means anything, he is just getting his wind up. Both his mother and his father lived to their 90s. Longevity, they say, runs in families.

—4—

Dan Berrigan's education as a Jesuit took place while World War II was being waged across North Africa, in Europe and in Asia. The wonder of those years for Berrigan, as he looks back now from a distance of several decades, is the lack of impact the war had on him philosophically and morally, both in terms of his existential self and his pacifist, antimilitary evolution. "We were just carried along with the war," he recalls. "The war was never a moral question."

Suspicion that World War II might not have been the just war almost everyone considered it to be was obviously trying to push through to Berrigan. He remembers, for instance, broaching to a class at St. Peter's Prep in Jersey City, his first teaching assignment, the proposition that before the atomic bomb was dropped on Japan the moral course would have been to carry out a demonstration bombing for the Japanese to alert them to the bomb's frightful power. He was shocked by an intensely negative reaction of his students; Hiroshima and Nagasaki were justified, they argued, on the principle that their obliteration saved American lives. It was for Berrigan a sobering education in the meaning of national chauvinism. Still it was without instant effect on him personally.

A year or two later, during theology studies at Weston College near Boston, Father John C. Ford, an eminent Jesuit thinker, raised the question of the morality of the saturation bombing of German cities. But Ford's lead was not pursued in particular depth, so that once again there was no jolting of Berrigan from the standard patriotic frame of mind to a sense that this so-called "good war" might be as evil as any other war ever fought.

Berrigan was at Woodstock during the final days of World War II, and he remembers a particularly bizarre incident after his brother Phil, a handsomely decorated infantry officer, arrived back from the European front. "V-J Day had just occurred, and Phil came down to see me, and the whole seminary organized a spontaneous victory demonstration," Berrigan recalls. There was a parade around the grounds—Phil, still in uniform, out front carrying a huge American flag, and the Jesuit seminarians strung out behind him, singing and cheering. "It was a really weird combination of emotions," says Berrigan. "I don't know what to say. National frenzy, of course. All of us had relatives in the war; some had relatives who had been killed. It was a great relief to have the war over. But there was no moral understanding of what this war, or any war, was all about. I guess that's what I'm trying to get at."

Today, Berrigan is convinced that World War II has led to every war since, and that in a horrible sense Hitler actually won World War II, because the United States and other countries have internationalized the spirit of those times and made mass extermination into a kind of international war method. "Even before Hiroshima, we were using the mass extermination methods of Hitler on German cities," Berrigan remarks, so in his mind there was in fact no giant ethical leap into Hiroshima once the A-bomb was ready. "So-called conventional weapons had been actually obliterating German cities, and nobody was saved, nobody was exempt. Even the children weren't—as they weren't at Hiroshima," he explains. "I feel that nothing in that so-called virtuous war can be justified, and that the only clue to another way of conduct was the manner in which certain of the occupied countries—the Scandinavian countries and to a degree Holland and France—resisted Hitler. That was by a nonviolent stopping of the show. But obviously that was not the method of the Great Powers."

Berrigan is not anxious to get hung up in argument over the fighting of World War II. "We can talk about those things interminably," he says. The relevant detail is that "at least the nuclear question has isolated the point that we are in a no-win situation now, whatever we think about the past." This does not mean, however, that Berrigan is non-judgmental about those who made the decision to drop the Bomb. This is Berrigan writing in his book *The Discipline of the Mountain:* "The President said calmly after the crime: We had the bomb and we used it. Years later, he died in his bed, by every indication at peace with his soul. The military leaders whose decision coincided with his own were queried years later for their memories of the event. Not one of them expressed regret. They stood in a closed circle."

"We are dealing with the antecedents of hell, not purgatory," Berrigan concluded bitterly.

Berrigan's stirring of conscience began after he was sent to France for a year's study in 1953, shortly after his ordination at Weston College by Boston's then archbishop, Richard J. Cushing. French theological thought and clerical example had had some influence on his thinking. He had nourished himself on Teilhard de Chardin, Henri de Lubac and Yves Congar. Paris's Cardinal Suhard, a guiding spirit of the Missions de France, was a special hero; so was Father Henri Perrin, the Jesuit who became a factory worker after surviving German concentration camps; so was Abbé Pierre, the Resistance leader who became a member of France's Chamber of Deputies and the motivating force behind a huge postwar housing program for the poor. Yet not even his acquaintance with French avant-garde thinkers and his affinity for doers on the French scene prepared Berrigan fully for the actual French experience. He said after his arrival in France that he felt like Br'er Rabbit being thrown into the briar patch. He was excited; he was stimulated; he felt as if he had landed on a new planet. "Something says 'I was born here,'" he wrote back. "Nothing like it on earth. The French for a steady diet are like Cognac before breakfast."

The conscience was stirring obviously, but full awakening was a time away. The 1953 Berrigan was still, in Berrigan's own judgment, an innocent abroad. Here he was defending the altruism of American foreign-aid programs; defending the execution of the Rosenbergs as traitors to the United States; dashing off to Germany as an auxiliary military chaplain preaching, hearing confessions, giving retreats to American soldiers. Such memories cause him to shudder now. "I was at a very strange, retarded stage," he declares.

France's people—notably priest-workers whose writings he knew and whose friendships he now cultivated—and events in France were inexorably at work on him. The major political trauma was the dissolving of France's colonial empire in Indochina. "I was witnessing the end of a totally hopeless war," he says of France's last days in Vietnam. "Even more important to me were the effects of that war on the home country. France was giving up on France because of that war. The French couldn't win that war; they couldn't get out of it until Dien Bien Phu. It was total chaos at home, and I remember French Jesuits saying to me, 'France is finished. The only way France is going to survive is in French Canada. We're all done with because of that war.' Anyway, all that got to me." It would explode within him several years later when the United States took over France's impossible burden.

Also "getting to him" was the effectual suppression of the priest-worker movement in the winter of 1954 by Pope Pius XII—"our icebox pope," in Berrigan's words. Berrigan, like so many liberal Catholics, had strong misgivings over Pius's 1950 encyclical, *Humani Generis,* which he considered aimed at the innovative thought of Teilhard de Chardin and other eminent French theologians. But that did not prepare him for the quashing of the priest-workers. "I saw at close hand intellectual excellence crushed in a wave of orthodoxy, like a big Stalinist purge," he was to reflect later. "It hit me directly; it made me suffer deeply; it filled me with determination to carry on the work of the men who had been silenced."

So it was that Berrigan, although still in ideological revolution, returned from France a markedly different man. Berrigan was not yet the radicalized priest, but he was moving in radically new directions. The next assignment brought a further development of the new man.

Berrigan was sent to Brooklyn Prep as a teacher of French and philosophy, and across the East River in Lower Manhattan was the Nativity Mission Center, which the Jesuits still have on Forsyth Street. The center was a point for social outreach, especially to Hispanics, and Berrigan brought students there on a regular basis as volunteers for the various programs. At the same time he had begun to work closely with the local unit of the Young Christian Workers, as well as with the Walter Farrell Guild, an organization which sought to upgrade the laity's role in the church. These groups broadened Berrigan's contacts with young people and provided more recruits for the programs in social justice going on in the area.

As fate would have it, nearby the Nativity Center, over on Christie Street, was the Catholic Worker house. The house inevitably became a stopping-off place. Berrigan had come under the influence of the Catholic Worker as a youth through the penny-a-copy *Catholic Worker* newspaper to which his father subscribed from its earliest days in 1933; he would now come directly in contact with Dorothy Day, that majestically inspirational woman who had founded the Catholic Worker movement with Peter Maurin and whose life by the 1950s had become a virtual personification of the corporal works of mercy. She had become a legend feeding the hungry, clothing the naked, sheltering the homeless, consoling the sick, burying the dead, visiting the imprisoned . . . and occasionally being a prisoner herself on behalf of justice and human rights. The effect of Dorothy Day and the Catholic Worker on Berrigan was dramatic and quickened regrets that a process in Catholic Worker sensitivity begun under the father had been interrupted during his years of training as a Jesuit. The focuses of the Worker—the humane practicalness of its concerns, its directness in the way it did things—all this appealed to him, and much of all this he would one day make his own, including taking on the Worker's pacifist position on war.

The just-war theory then enjoyed almost unchallenged acceptance in Catholic theological circles, and Berrigan credits Dorothy Day and the Catholic Worker with getting him out of intellectual "swaddling clothes" and into an adult understanding that a just war is a contradiction in terms, a perversion of logic, and that any war, conven-

tional or nuclear, is an obscenity, a crime against humanity, a profaning of the gospel admonitions. It is an understanding, he says, that he would never have received in his
order. Indeed, Berrigan bristles when he thinks of the
"good-natured contempt" that for decades defined attitudes within the Jesuit order toward Dorothy Day and
the Worker, especially on the question of war. "If only
Dorothy would stick to her last, like a good shoemaker,
and leave these big questions to us. . . . She's really admira-
ble, and she's making soup for the poor, but she doesn't
know the intricacies." That sort of academic comment, that
clerical contempt soured Berrigan. To him, Dorothy Day
was infinitely more worthy of respect than her critics.
Dorothy Day and the Catholic Worker helped peel away
what Berrigan calls some "awful mild theology."

Another benefit the Worker provided was bringing him
further in touch with types he has admired most all his life,
gospel-oriented young men and women with the willingness to question the system and the spunk to act out of
conscientious convictions. Berrigan witnessed the marriages of young Catholic Workers, rapped with them during many a Friday night colloquy, a feature of the Catholic
Worker house, and performed the Eucharist for them on
any number of occasions.

Dorothy Day, much the liturgical traditionalist, once
complained about one of these liturgies to Dwight Macdonald, the writer, in being interviewed for an essay that
appeared in *The New York Review of Books*. The liturgy was
rather orthodox by Berrigan standards. Out of deference
for Dorothy, it did not include, for instance, readings from
Pablo Neruda, W. H. Auden, T. S. Eliot, or others whom
Berrigan might have thought appropriate for the occasion. For the consecration, however, he used a loaf of

French bread, "tore off hunks with his hands, crumbs all over the floor." According to Dorothy, these crumbs were later "swept up and dumped into the garbage pail," an action that greatly disturbed her. "If you really believe they had become the flesh of Jesus, as I do literally," she said, "well, that was no way to treat the body of Our Lord. Those crumbs bothered me."

Berrigan professes not to remember the incident as vividly as Dorothy did to Macdonald, but he is apologetic nonetheless. "I'm sure there was an occasion like that," he allows. "I would have to say as I look back that I was very insensitive to the deep, deep feelings of a great person. These matters are sacred and should be handled very carefully. I guess I was in some other orbit at the time. But I'm much more careful when I go back now, and have been for years." He adds with respect to liturgical carefulness that this is general policy, not just when he is celebrating the Eucharist at the Worker.

However, nothing of this puts Berrigan in a line of conformity with the new regulations from the Vatican's Congregation for the Sacraments and Divine Liturgy aimed at curbing latitudes being taken by priests within the liturgy. In a public situation, Berrigan tends to do what other clerics do, "hoping it would be simple." But he much prefers a liturgy that is intimate and spontaneous. He described in the spring of 1980 a liturgy held a day or two before at Jonah House, the resistence-community center established in Baltimore by his brother Philip and Philip's wife Elizabeth. "We had a rather extended scripture reading and discussion and silence. Then I improvised the Eucharist. That's all." The word "improvised" is Berrigan's, but the sense may be somewhat misleading. Berrigan always uses the formal words of consecration—

"because that's scriptural," he says. The readings and sur-
rounding prayers? "Well," says Berrigan, "I try to take
leads from what we have just been through, or what we
have discussed, or our friends, or the people in jail."

The "people in jail" reference particularizes the Berrigan liturgy in unique ways. It is a reference that testifies to
the regard Berrigan has for the outcasts of society. And in
a special way it is a reference that honors political prisoners, those in jail for having the courage of their convictions and from whose witness Berrigan's liturgies seek to
draw strength and insight. At any given time, these imprisoned people could be family—not just the extended
family of the human community, but blood brothers and a
sister-in-law: Phil and Elizabeth, of course, and more recently his brother Jerry. Jerry, now turned 60, is a professor of English at Onondaga Community College in Syracuse; he is a one-time Josephite seminarian, husband and
father of four adopted children. Cut from the same
ideological cloth as his younger brothers, and with his own
children pretty well grown, Jerry launched into activism
involving civil disobedience when he was in his 50s, being
arrested for the first time in 1973 with Dan during a pray-
in at the White House. There were subsequent arrests in
1976 and 1980. When I interviewed him, he was on a
30-days' suspended sentence and six-months' probation on
charges of depredation of government property during a
demonstration at the Pentagon, Defense Department
headquarters in Arlington, Virginia, which the Berrigans
call a "temple of death/murder."

The 1976 arrest found not only Jerry, but all four of the
activist Berrigan clan in jail at one time. Jerry, Dan, Phil,
and Elizabeth had joined with 150 others in a demonstra-

tion at the Pentagon. The day was December 28, the Feast of the Massacre of the Innocents, a day of special meaning in the Berrigan calendar. For years the Berrigans have made the Feast of the Massacre of the Innocents a focus for action, and in 1976 there seemed extra reason for doing something. Mother Berrigan, Frida, had died just before Christmas, and as a tribute to her memory the four had decided on a family witness at the Pentagon. It developed that all four were arrested—Dan and Jerry for blocking an entrance; Phil and Elizabeth for defacing government property. Dan and Jerry had chained themselves to a door; Phil and Liz had spread about blood and ashes, symbolic of the fate they consider the world's if the arms race goes on.

For Dan and Jerry, the arrests were not unduly complicating of their home lives, but for Phil and Elizabeth it was another story. Elizabeth received a stiff six-months' sentence, later reduced to 90 days; Phil got a total of 70 days. This meant that two infant children were suddenly deprived of both mother and father. Frida, their first born, was not yet three; Jerry, not yet two. At Jonah House, the children were among responsible, loving people. Still, for children that young, the separation from parents was extremely unsettling, perhaps even traumatic. The children survived without observable scars. In fact, says Phil, "after we came home, they were just very happy to see everyone." The children may even have begun to come to an understanding at that point, he adds, that this separation would perhaps be something of a pattern, an impression borne out for him by the courageous way the children endured their mother's last stay in prison: 30 days in early 1980, again for disrupting business at the

Pentagon. Nevertheless, the parents resolved after the 1976 experience that never again would the two of them be in jail at the same time—"if we can help it."

—5—

The concept of family is holy to any parent. It is holy to Dan Berrigan, who is not a parent. Neither a father's ill temper nor stinging denunciation by two older brothers—which was to come during the Vietnam resistance period—has ever been allowed to disturb that concept. "That's where I come from, everything I have," Dan Berrigan has said of family (in *U.S. Catholic*). "It's where my bonds are tightest. . . . This has been, practically speaking, my great strength, both my family and the Jesuits."

The Berrigan farm in Liverpool has been subdivided, much of the acreage being given over to suburban development. The homestead of Tom Berrigan's family, which passed to Tom and Frida as the original Berrigan clan thinned and died, is in other hands. It was sold in the early '70s for a token sum to an interracial couple and their children. "We were so glad," says Berrigan. "It seemed so fitting." And indeed it was; Tom Berrigan had helped found Syracuse's first Catholic Interracial Council.

Though the old habitats are gone, and the parents dead, Syracuse remains a kind of family center for the current clan of Berrigans. Home base now is brother Jerry's and wife Carol's place, a comfortable low-slung house crammed with books and Berrigan memorabilia. It is where Dan's medals, citations, and souvenirs of the activist life arrive, to go up on the wall alongside other family mementos, like framed dust jackets of Dan's and Phil's books. It is where, as if to refresh the spirit, Dan visits regularly, often on a detour from one or another speaking engagement or mission of witness.

It is easy for a Berrigan to get in touch with roots here. Out back, beyond Jerry's mountains of firewood and his ambitious vegetable garden—organic, of course—Loretto Geriatric Center rises high over the neighborhood of middle-class houses. Frida and Tom Berrigan spent their last years there, and from there their spirit reaches out these several years after their deaths to the home of their son. Jerry's house—the work sheds, those stacks of wood piled as neat as sheets in a linen closet—speak loudly of the father. In interests and talents about the house, Jerry Berrigan is very much his father's son, and Dan can be almost envious at times that the skills of the father in gardening, carpentry, plumbing, and other manual trades slipped by him.

The Berrigan brothers form what has been whimsically described as a double troika: John, Tom, and Jim, the oldest three, comprising one team; Jerry, Dan, and Phil, the other. Sectioning off within families is a natural thing, and probably more so when there is a lot of heavy work to be done and this is divided according to the strength of the youngsters to handle it; older brothers are always stronger, at least to start with. It does not necessarily mean that because some are closer to others than to all that they are less caring or loving of all in the family. So it proved in the Berrigan family, although for a time it seemed the case would be otherwise.

The brotherly solidarity of the Berrigans received its great testing in February, 1971 when John gave an embittered press interview in which he labeled the antiwar activities of his two youngest brothers "detrimental" to the United States. Tom's feelings, which also became public, turned out to be of a kind. Only Jim of the senior troika was not avowedly anti-Dan and anti-Phil. The disavowal of brothers by brothers occurred while Dan and Phil were behind bars in Danbury, and hurt deeply. Nor did animosity quick dissipate itself. Antipathy persisted, then hardened when Phil married. For John and Tom, the marriage of their priest-brother capped the tragedy of events.

Throughout this family crisis, Dan refused to take as a final insult any affront that was directed at him, and his patience was rewarded. The breach closed bit by bit, with final reconciliation being achieved around the death of Tom's wife Honor in 1979. Tom had never met Elizabeth McAlister (she retained her surname when she married), had never wanted to. He had never seen Elizabeth's and Phil's children. He had cut them all off. During Honor's illness, the family gathered about the Eucharist in Tom's home in Providence, Rhode Island. Phil and Liz remained down in Baltimore, uninvited. Finally, with Honor dying—dear Honor, who had been an Anglican, who had different ideas about celibacy and the clergy, who had never severed Phil and Elizabeth from her life—the two said, "We're just going up there and see her." They did, not even knowing whether the door would be opened to them. It was. Forgiveness flowed, the tensions of years melted away, and the Berrigan brothers were once again the united gang they were back on the farm in Liverpool. When Dan's book *The Discipline of the Mountain* appeared that same year, it was dedicated "in loving memory" to Honor.

The marriage of Phil and Elizabeth—entered into by "mutual consent" in the spring of 1969, later formalized, and made public on May 28, 1973—was a test not only for the brother Tom. "It was a very tough thing at the time for everyone in the family," says Dan, "especially for my mother." But she accepted and adjusted, thanks to what he and his brothers term her wonderful capacity for growth. Today Elizabeth McAlister is prized as a great blessing in the Berrigan family, an enrichment for everyone—for reason of herself; for the new blood she has brought into the family with young Frida and young Jerry; and for what the senior Jerry says is the way she "served to specify and crystalize in our minds issues of the individual conscience vis-à-vis official church teaching by bringing the matter home to us in the life of a family member who is a priest and decided to marry." Dan adds his tribute: "I think I told Phil once, and maybe I told both Phil and Liz, that they don't really dictate to me the way my life goes, because in many ways my life is very, very different. But they're like a landmark or North Star. I can take soundings by them of general directions that I should be taking, and they never allow me to forget 'first things first'—which I think I could get too easygoing about."

Today there is no discomfort whatsoever in the Berrigan family over Phil's status. Quite the opposite. Phil, who has refused to laicize, considers himself as much a priest today as the day in 1950 when he was ordained a Josephite. The family is at ease with that, preferring to believe with Phil that there should be room within the church for a noncelibate as well as a celibate clergy. This is an abrupt about-face for Phil from a position once defended. Originally he held celibacy to be an essential condition for the revolutionary, as it enabled him to devote himself unqualifiedly to his struggle. He changed his mind on that, but not to the extent that he would belittle the celibacy ideal. "Celibacy is a great tradition," he holds, "but only if it is an enhancement of human freedom and rights.

Unless celibacy is optional and constantly renewed for very personal and public reasons, it becomes useless. The spirit of freedom is destroyed." His brother Dan subscribes to that. Indeed, Dan is convinced yet that officials in the church squandered a bright opportunity for development and growth when they expelled Phil from his order instead of using the situation of his having married to focus new elements of hope and insight on religious life and the institution of Christian marriage. The Josephites lost no time expelling Phil from the order once they got news of his marriage. Dan termed the expulsion "outrageous." "I see it as a sign of the retardation of religious life that some of the best people continue to be forced out of religious communities," he said. "In a profound sense, it is a kind of working out of the death wish of these orders." He would say the same today, believing more than ever that "whatever future religious life has is bound up with optional celibacy."

As Berrigan would expand the possibilities of religious life, so would he create new models of family life. His own strong family ties notwithstanding, and notwithstanding also his admiration for the families his brothers have and are raising, he is not persuaded that the traditional model completely serves a new age. He would opt for something quite different.

What bothers Berrigan is that the traditional, so-called nuclear family is in the same impasse he considers the churches to be: it isn't changing; it is tied to the consumer cycle; worst yet, it stifles growth and search among young people because young married couples, as members of the prevailing social community, suddenly must give up activism for work and regimentation and acceptance, becoming in the process more dependent on and vulnerable to the power of a town, a city, a county, a state, a country. This point of view is not a recent one. In 1966, he broached the subject in his book *They Call Us Dead Men*. He wrote that the social aspect of marriage as a perfective of society had been largely neglected, and the proof of this neglect was to be found, he said, in the tentative nature of the ventures made by married couples, and specifically Catholics, in the social arena, as well as in the magnitude of the tasks shied away from. "Catholic couples are armed to the teeth with prayer and the sacraments, but they find themselves largely bewildered before the chaos of fermenting hope and despair in the world at large," he remarked.

Returning to the subject of the family in 1971 in the long, taped conversation with Harvard psychiatrist Robert Coles published as the book *The Geography of Faith,* Berrigan argued that couples "must explore ways of sharing talents, of sharing in the rearing of children, the care of the home, the earning of money."

In essence, Berrigan plumbs for a family situation in which husband and wife can maintain their sense of privacy with the children, yet at the same time can pursue a political course which they think necessary and important. It would be a family situation in which young people growing up have before them a wide variety of possibilities—where the children know well many kinds of people, and not just the two people who begot them; where they have exposure from the earliest years to what Berrigan has called "models of manhood."

Berrigan is convinced that too many families are like armies, where children are segregated, indoctrinated, isolated in order to be injected with a worldview. "Armies, and all too many homes and schools, discourage real freedom of expression, freedom to think broadly, roam widely through books and ideas," he comments. "And armies succeed, as do many of our homes and schools; lives are controlled, spirits crushed, wars of one kind or another waged and won. But children pay for these victories. We all do. We become indifferent and self-centered—the very enemy of Christ's spirit of sacrifice and love for all mankind."

If not a precise model, then certainly a reflection of the type of family situation Berrigan has in mind would be that which exists at Jonah House, where Phil and Elizabeth are raising their children. In the physical sense, Jonah House is typically Baltimore: a brick rowhouse, four floors including basement, and up and down the street white marble stairs out front, which people do indeed scrub. In spirit, on the other hand, Jonah House is anything but typical. Located in an interracial neighborhood of whites, blacks, and Orientals, Jonah House survives on the industry and ingenuity of its members—11 adults and three children. Not all are there at one time, which is just as well; there are rooms for but eight adults. Phil, Elizabeth, and their children occupy the two basement rooms—the children sharing their space with a hot-air furnace (which they use as a bulletin board); Phil and Liz sharing theirs with washer, dryer, work bench, carpentry tools, and ladders slung on brackets fixed to the wall above the head of their double bed. The ladders, horizontal to the floor, become convenient bookcases when not otherwise in use. That would be in the cold-weather months only.

Every Jonah House adult works, generally at painting and roofing jobs. "We're cheap, and we do reasonably good work," says Phil. "The word gets around." Income from the jobs goes far in keeping the house going. Even the women work, although Elizabeth draws the line on heights of more than 24 feet. One or two days a week, a team will break away from the current work project and scrounge the giant food and produce depot at Jessup, between Baltimore and Washington, for vegetables and fruits, breads and pastries which are being discarded because of over-supply, over-ripeness, or a border-line date for commercial sale. The Jonah House people keep what they need, and the remainder they distribute to a soup kitchen serving the poor, as well as to the poor of the neighborhood. Many families have thus come to be dependent on Jonah House in small but significant ways. The day of my visit, a man appeared at the door to say he hadn't gotten his two loaves of bread that morning when the Jonah House truck arrived back from its run; actually his son had picked the bread up, but who was to argue? "You'd be amazed at what's thrown into the dumpsters," says Elizabeth. "Perfectly good food, like heads of lettuce whose outside leaves may be gone by, but which are fine inside." The salad on the table was made from lettuce salvaged the week before.

Jonah House has another purpose, however, in addition to the mere welfare of its occupants and the good of its neighbors. Jonah House is a community striving to get back to the roots of religious and resistance tradition and translate that to the American scene in hopes of bringing the country to a new sense of human priorities. Its members seek to do this through prayer and meditation, through study of the gospels and the works of writers like Gandhi, Tolstoy, and Daniel Berrigan, and through demonstrations of concern at places like the White House and the Pentagon, where the future is being determined hour by hour in what the Jonah House people see as evil and perverse ways. They are convinced that time is running out for humankind, and that the future has been mortgaged to the "warmakers," whose rhetoric, they say, promises peace but results rather in more and more weapons systems: MX missiles, Trident submarines, cruise missiles, neutron bombs, first-strike weapons. Jonah House's position is essentially that of the French writer and Nobel laureate, Albert Camus. "All I ask," Camus once said, "is that, in the midst of a murderous world, we agree to reflect on murder and make a choice." The Jonah House people have reflected and made their choice. It is for a future for children, a future where there will be food for the hungry and shelter for the homeless, a future in which humankind does not have to live under the Bomb and in fear of the morrow. Dan Berrigan obviously is at home in Jonah House. He endorses it as a home for his niece and nephew.

The concept for Jonah House came out of the Catholic peace community and the resistance to the war in Vietnam, which Dan and Phil Berrigan spearheaded in ways some would say imaginative, some would say unsavory. The guidelines were worked out mostly from jail, where Phil spent long years for his opposition to the war, and at meetings in New York City, which Elizabeth held with members of the Harrisburg Defense Committee, the support group in the 1972 trial of herself and her husband and five other peace activists for an alleged conspiracy to kidnap presidential adviser Henry A. Kissinger and blow up heating tunnels to federal buildings in Washington, D.C. Essentially, Jonah House is conceived as a response to a question that to them became pertinent as the Vietnam war died out and the country went back to business as usual: "What do we learn from the past as action communities and how do we carry that into the future?" Jonah House's method, subscribed to and joined in by Dan, although he himself lives elsewhere, is to work for peace by focusing attention on the preoccupation with armaments. This makes the Pentagon a natural object of concern. Their logic is unambiguous. "The Pentagon is the largest single employer in the world," Dan Berrigan comments. "The people who work there stand for one of every two engineers and scientists in the country. It's absolutely unimaginable. If we want to look at the spiritual results of all this, we are being enlisted into a scene of permanent violence and warfare."

Jonah House demonstrations outside the Pentagon have been going on for more than six years now, and although arms production continues at an unrestrained clip, those carrying the challenge to the Pentagon believe they can see subtle changes. "The atmosphere in the Pentagon has changed radically toward people like ourselves," says Dan Berrigan, as reported in *U.S. Catholic.* "They're listening instead of deriding and catcalling. When we put on one of our powerful shows and pour our blood around and throw ashes, the whole place looks like a slaughterhouse. The people don't react anymore as if this is some kind of cheap show biz. They act a little bit as if it's something about their fate. When we were there in Holy Week (1980), the bosses had to get bullhorns and order people back to work—and they were very slow in going back."

It is important to note in the Berrigans-McAlister context that none of their demonstrations or actions is entered into without spiritual preparation. This applies whether they are acting as a small group or, as is getting to be more and more the case, in concert with peace communities coming from as far away as Nashville, Toronto, Hartford, or the Lehigh Valley. Says Dan Berrigan: "We never go into one of these actions without a period of prayer. If it's possible, a weekend of prayer with the whole group, not just those who plan to be civilly disobedient, but everyone, because we try to welcome people at various stages. People may just want to leaflet. People may want to be there to pray. They may want to watch. We want everybody who's going to be with us, whether at the Riverside Research Institute in New York, or the Pentagon, or the White House, to take part in a period of community sharing and prayer. We have never said, 'Meet me at 9 a.m. at the Pentagon.' We start from the church. The church is the place you go from—which is an interesting definition we borrowed from Martin Luther King. It's not the place you stay in. It's the place you go from. After we pray together, what follows—civil disobedience or whatever—is not just a spasm. It's a result of the prayer. Now we are publicly responsible for what we have prayed about."

As it is in 1980, so was it in the 1960s and 1970s when the Berrigans gave civil disobedience a new definition in the United States.

2
The Decade That Made Activist History

—1—

The decade of the 1960s was the great activist decade in the social history of the United States—the time in which the country's eyes were opened to its invisible poor, thanks largely to a president's reading of a book by Michael Harrington, *The Other America;* the time in which the country was confronted at last by a black population seething like a Mount St. Helens under two centuries of exploitation, discrimination, and deprivation.

The beginnings of the 1960s found Daniel Berrigan back in Syracuse, near family, which was pleasant, and busy as a professor in New Testament studies at LeMoyne College, which was challenging. He had been assigned to LeMoyne in 1957 from Brooklyn Prep, and through the assignment involved him in a whole new teaching field at a new and more demanding educational level, he found his interests again being drawn from the precincts of academe to the world beyond.

Berrigan did not have to be hit on the head with the perceptions of John F. Kennedy's new national administration to appreciate the issues of the 1960s. As early as March, 1958 he was speaking out on deplorable housing conditions on Syracuse's lower east side, and bearding bankers and real-estate owners for their part in the perpetuation of slum conditions and for drawing as hard and fast a line across the paths of blacks in Syracuse as had ever been drawn in the Deep South. The criticism did not sit well with college officials, as some of the targets of his criticism were members of the college's board of trustees, helping to build the college itself. LeMoyne was then still an infant institution; it dates only from 1946. In the minds of Berrigan's superiors, it was not a time for boat-rocking. But to Berrigan compromise was as impossible as indifference. It was apparent to him, he said later, that if he hoped to survive in a campus situation it would have to be in conflict against that dependency on the powerful and the rich which diverted the institution from human ideals, including serving the poor.

Berrigan did not remake LeMoyne or Syracuse, but people in the area certainly knew he was around—and other Berrigans as well. Jerry was back in Syracuse, having left the Josephite seminary a year short of ordination. Dan, Jerry, and Jerry's young bride Carol joined in picketing against discriminatory hiring practices at Niagara-Mohawk electric company, the company for which their father once worked. Phil by this time had been ordained a Josephite and was teaching and counseling at St. Augustine High School in New Orleans. He and Dan began an exchange program that had LeMoyne students going south in the summer to share in Phil's work among very poor blacks, and graduates of St. Augustine's coming north on scholarships to LeMoyne. "That was a good start," Dan remarks.

Meanwhile, Dan was organizing a community of students off-campus that was a kind of precursor of the Peace Corps. This would have been around 1960. "We got an OK from the college to set up our own house and have our own liturgy, and our own life together," says Berrigan. The students—some 15 or so—were drawn from the intellectually elite; the governing stipulation was that they were to keep up first-rate work in college and give the summer to work in Mexico among the poor. That was all very new for those days, and Berrigan takes satisfaction that the work is still going on. The initiative in Syracuse grew into International House and Berrigan was designated director. From the Trappist Abbey at Gethsemani, Merton sent a piece of signed art to place in the living room as a blessing on the house. Tom Berrigan, the father, still very much alive, came around to build an altar for the chapel.

The liturgies celebrated on this altar quickly became something of a cause célèbre. The altar was constructed so that Mass could be offered facing the people. That was innovation, but not nearly so innovative as Berrigan's introducing of the vernacular into the liturgy. This was two and three years before Vatican Council II provided for a vernacular liturgy. Just to say the *Gloria* in English was then a startling departure from tradition. The older Jesuits were "horrified," Berrigan remembers, but it was the young people about whose reaction he cared. They were enthusiastic. "The kids and I felt that for the first time in a thousand years we were building community around the altar," he declares.

At the same time, Berrigan was building community between himself and former students of his who had gone on to the Jesuits. The medium was letters, some of them unsigned and obviously meant to be shared by the wider seminary student body. "He was a mentor to many people," remarks Joseph Mendola, a novice in Poughkeepsie from 1963–65 and now a clinical psychologist working in the Boston area. "His letters were as epistles to young Jesuits. They drove the older Jesuits wild, but for many of us they were a means of staying humane and human." One missive; which characterized the priesthood as a "sheepfold for sheep" and which sketched new concepts of ministry and redemption, became an instant favorite of the seminarians' underground. In it, Berrigan spoke of his ordination nine years before: "I rose to my feet and went out into the sunshine and gave my blessing to those who had borne with me, who had waited for me. A most unfinished man! What would it mean to be a Catholic? Who would be my teacher? It was, finally, the world. It was the world we breathe in, the only stage of redemption, the men and women who toil in it, sin in it, suffer and die in it. Apart from them, as I came to know, the priesthood was a pallid, vacuumatic enclosure, a sheepfold for sheep." In time—after the liberating impact of Pope John XXIII—the essay became something of a Jesuit classic, being reprinted by the thousands and assigned to novices' reading lists. But in 1961 it smacked of subversion; the world was the devil.

Indeed, it was not only into Jesuit seminaries that the Berrigan influence was reaching. Father Frank J. Iazzetta, pastor of Holy Trinity Church in Long Branch, New Jersey reviews his years at Immaculate Conception Seminary in Darlington during the 1960s, and says Berrigan was a strong influence there and on seminary life generally in the United States. "He was very influential on seminary change; in fact, he was actually essential to it," says Iazzetta. Seminarians chafing under outdated rules and unbending authority sought Berrigan out and were told to stick to conscience, to contemporize themselves, to work against oppressions. Iazzetta ticks off some of the "oppressions": no newspapers, no entering each other's room, extremely limited contact with family. "It was a real violence that they were doing to us, as far as he was concerned," says Iazzetta. He credits Berrigan with indirectly putting Darlington and other American seminaries under such pressure of revolt from within that they had no choice but to ease regulations so that seminary students could come to what Iazzetta calls "a contemporary understanding of society."

Seminary directors were infuriated over what they considered an alien, intrusive influence on seminary life and training. But the course of history—church history at least—belonged to people of the Berrigan vision, and less and less to those of the old school.

In American society, meanwhile, the civil-rights struggle, so intense in the South, was creeping northward. The Montgomery bus boycott of 1955–56 had given way to lunch-counter sit-ins in 1960, and suddenly there was hardly a city in the country immune to integration history. The first of the sit-ins was at F.W. Woolworth's in Greensboro, North Carolina. Woolworth stores were everywhere, including Syracuse, and students from Syracuse University quickly descended on the local store of the company in a sympathy demonstration with what was happening in Greensboro. It was obvious to anyone with eyes to see that fevers of indignation were likely to leap from one campus to another. LeMoyne's rector acted decisively. Berrigan and others like him were not to do anything exotic like those crazies at Syracuse University who were picketing and sitting-in at Woolworths over the refusal of service to blacks in the South. Berrigan, still working out mounting interior conflicts between conscience and authority, restrained himself.

It was less easy the next time, in 1963. Phil, now stationed at the Josephite Seminary in Newburgh, New York proposed that the two of them join in a Freedom Ride to protest the segregation of bus terminals in Jackson, Mississippi. A mass sit-in was planned, and each wanted to be part of it. Dan went to see the Jesuit provincial in Buffalo to ask permission to go. Berrigan was hopeful. The provincial was a man with a reputation for decency and fairness. When Berrigan presented his proposal, however, he got a flat rejection. "I can remember the scene well," Berrigan said in 1980, 17 years later. "I laid this whole thing out and I was given thumbs down in a really bad way. He became very stiff-necked. We couldn't go into the territory of other bishops without their permission, and there would be no question of my going on such a project." Phil pressed on independently with the plan, hopping a plane from New York to Atlanta, to connect there for Jackson. He got no further. In Atlanta he was paged to a telephone and ordered back by his superior. The bishop of Jackson, he was told, had complained to the Josephite superior that if Father Philip Berrigan came to Jackson he would make a complaint directly to Rome. Phil turned back, but not without some small measure of satisfaction. The press was alerted to what was happening and the incident made front pages in newspapers across much of the country. The press correctly saw the incident as the joining of the civil-rights crisis in the American Catholic church.

The confrontation in Buffalo left Dan Berrigan shaken, and his superiors leery of the man they had on their hands. Back in Syracuse, he was summoned over to the rector's "think table," a spot in the rector's study to which problem clerics were called for talking to, counseling, and disciplining. It was decided that Berrigan would take a sabbatical in France. In fact Berrigan came near to taking a walk out of the order, and it was the letter from Merton, mentioned earlier, that persuaded him to stay. Though the letter calmed Berrigan, it probably also enlarged his sense of indignation over the restraints under which clergymen were forced to labor by including a recitation of grievances which Merton himself was laboring under.

"Look," wrote Merton, "a lot of the monastic party line we are getting ends up by being pure, unadulterated—crap. In the name of lifeless letters on parchment we are told that our life consists in the pious meditation on scriptures and withdrawal from the world. Try anything serious and immediately you get the line 'activist' thrown at you. I have been told that I am destroying the image of the contemplative vocation when I write about peace. Even after *Pacem in Terris,* when I reopened the question, I was told: 'That is for the bishops, my boy.' In a word, it is all right for the monk to break his ass putting out packages of cheese and making a pile of money for the old monastery, but to do anything really fruitful for the church, that is another matter altogether. . . ."

However, Merton concluded his letter to Berrigan with advice to go to Europe. It is "obviously the next step," he wrote, "because over there you may find out what's what. And you need to. When you do, let me know." Berrigan heeded.

Berrigan's friendship with Merton was crucial at this point in his life, and indeed continued to be right up to December 10, 1968, when Merton died in that bizarre accident with an electric fan in Bangkok, Thailand. Berrigan and Merton had first come in contact in 1948 after the appearance of *The Seven Storey Mountain,* Merton's autobiographical account of family life and the influences that led him to convert to Catholicism and become a Trappist. The book was a sensational success, and it enthralled Berrigan as it did tens of thousands of others. Berrigan wrote warmly to Merton of the book, and received back a prayer card with a small message on it. Monks were under a communications' discipline then quite stricter than what was to be the case later. Their correspondence thus languished, but was renewed with vigor after an article of Merton's on nuclear weapons appeared in the *Catholic Worker*. Merton, a pacifist, a disciple of nonviolence, was under a darkening pessimism that a permanent peace could ever be established in the world. His mood, his reading of the world situation, shook Berrigan, who sat down that very day and wrote Merton. By that time—it was now 1959—Merton was able to correspond more freely, and a friendship blossomed. There was a steady flow of letters back and forth and visits together at Gethsemani that took the form of retreats and meditations on witness, the spiritual roots of protest, and the art of nonviolence. Kindred souls joined them, including Phil Berrigan, James Forest, Robert Cunnane, Thomas Cornell, all Catholic peace activists and all eventually imprisoned for antiwar activities of various kinds.

Berrigan and Merton were as brothers. They had their differences of viewpoint. Berrigan, for instance, once charged Merton with "leading a whole generation into the cloister whom you'll never lead out." He believed passionately that one had to be in the world in order to have a strong grip on it. Merton, on the other hand, is believed to have been quite dubious about the aggressive nonviolence eventually adopted by Berrigan. Still, they were men of a mind with one another, and theirs was a friendship that was "very dear" to Berrigan. "I think probably I was his closest friend," Berrigan says of those last years of Merton's life, although, he adds, "I wouldn't make a big deal of that." What was important, says Berrigan, was that "there were times in his life when I was able to cast him a lifeline, and he did it for me," as in 1963.

When Merton died, Berrigan was grief-stricken. He took to the streets of New York, wandering aimlessly. He put his feelings into poetry:

> Friend, between Bangkok and this
> new year zeroing in, how death
> abounds, for those who try and try
>
> the odds you took and tossed, on life!
> Coffee and hamburg in a Greek hash joint
> alone; a Bogie double feature. Winds stir
>
> dead news in the street, frenzy, bombast. Meat
> sticks in my throat. The gravel voice
> of dead Bogart
>
> cheats like a virtuous thief
> usurious times.
> Merton . . .

In 1970, when he published *No Bars to Manhood,* Berrigan dedicated the book to "my father, Thomas Berrigan; my brother, Thomas Merton."

—2—

The France that Berrigan found in 1963 was not the France that he left in 1954, although not so startlingly different as some writers have portrayed it as being for him. The worst of the Algerian war was over, the Indochina war was a bitter and brutal memory, and France had begun a real march toward prosperity—and toward the nuclear club. In a sense, France of the 1960s was the United States of the 1950s, which may be the effect that old soldiers have as leaders of a nation's people; France's de Gaulle was America's Eisenhower. There was less poverty, more complacency, and a growing middle class. If Berrigan did not feel greatly challenged by the scene, he also was not turned off entirely. The priest-workers, after having been crushed under Pius XII, were slowly recovering under Pope John XXIII, albeit with more Roman control. Berrigan grew very close to a group of worker-priests in the workers' area of Paris, a parish called St. Hippolyte. His essential work, however, was with students, and although he forged friendships that lasted for a good many years, the experience was less than stimulating. Berrigan is mildly sardonic in recalling the time. "Unfortunately," he says, "I was earning my living that year as a chaplain in a student house on the Left Bank. I was mainly dealing with about a hundred middle-class, Catholic university people—and I did not have a great deal of rapport with them, I must say."

Inevitably, Berrigan's eyes turned from a France that he found more and more homogenized from an American point of view to Eastern Europe, then still in the early throes of national Communisms. He resolved to go there to see, in his words, "how Christians were making it in very different circumstances than I had known." It would also be an opportunity to test certain presumptions that had crept into his mind with respect to Western, so-called Christian civilization, including the suspicion that the west was moving in a direction which was not qualitatively different from that of the adversary it berated and armed against. "It is clear that we retain at least to some degree that sense of man and of God that has marked the history of Western man," he had declared the year before at the 1962 Liturgical Week. "But even this concession is in need of careful analysis. The moral attitudes of the West are, in fact, growing progressively less reasoned, less commonly assumed, and more sentimental. We are a benevolent people without knowing quite why. Social altruism seems to suit our character and is identified widely with us, but neither we nor our critics think commonly or realistically of explaining our compassion and generosity as being governed by religious conviction. Our mercy toward enemies, our hatred of violence, our energetic respect for good works—these are less and less conspicuously connected with religious belief. Today, they are generally studied and explained in terms of ethos, sentimental humanism, or world expediency."

Nothing of his trips behind the Iron Curtain persuaded Berrigan that his reading of the West was wrong. The Marxist states were also as he expected them to be. But the faithful, the people of God—they were an inspiration. "The churches in the Marxist countries are small but purified by persecution," he said on his return. "It seems that God is cleaning up the old state-church arrangements. The Christians under Marxism have returned to their pre-Constantinian situation of being poor, pure, and persecuted, and they are leading the life which I believe God had decreed for the church." He liked what he saw, the Christians he met. "What a great feeling," he remarked, "to be in a country where there's no head of state going to church every Sunday and corrupting it!" The comment had an obvious American application.

Berrigan's first trip to Eastern Europe took him to Czechoslovakia and Hungary. It was a bit scary, given the times. Westerners were not wandering around those countries then in large numbers, certainly not Western clergymen, and perhaps least of all any who were Jesuits. Berrigan went alone, connected with friends in Prague, who put him in touch with friends of their own in Hungary. It was all very stimulating. Berrigan returned by way of Rome, anxious to share his observations with the Vatican, particularly with respect to Protestant Churches and the ways by which they were managing to survive in most difficult circumstances. His report amounted to a very strong recommendation on the part of the Protestant communities that the Vatican begin to take a more practical interest in the religious and social situation in Marxist Central Europe. Berrigan sat down with an assistant of Augustin Cardinal Bea, the Jesuit who headed the Vatican Secretariat for Promoting Christian Unity. The aide gave Berrigan a sympathetic hearing, but seemingly little more. "I was trying to interest the church officials in the idea that I should be appointed a Vatican observer at the Christian Peace Conference to be held [in Prague] in the summer of 1964," says Berrigan. "Alas for those great hopes."

Berrigan did get to the peace conference, however, and though the conference changed the course of very little—Berrigan was bored by 90 percent of it—it did by indirection spin off a new peace organization for the United States. Berrigan went to Prague in the company of Jim Forest from the New York Catholic Worker house, James Douglass, a layman pursuing theological studies in Rome, and John Heidbrink, a Presbyterian minister then close to the Catholic Worker and Catholic pacifists. The four talked for hours of the lack in the American Catholic community of an organization for the development of Catholic thought on questions of war and peace, and collectively decided that it was past time for an educational and action agency to fill the gap. They decided to found the Catholic Peace Fellowship, an organization that eventually was to win the support of several American bishops, counsel tens of thousands of Catholic conscientious objectors, and provide educational services for a number of Catholic school systems. In some respects, the Catholic Peace Fellowship was an offshoot of A. J. Muste's Fellowship of Reconciliation, a nondenominational peace group that had been around for years. But the Catholic Peace Fellowship aimed for an identity of its own, and succeeded in achieving one. Some of the most prominent members of the Catholic peace community—Dorothy Day, Thomas Merton, Philip Berrigan, among others—signed on as cochairpersons, so that the Catholic Peace Fellowship board became a veritable *Who's Who* of concerned American Catholics. Forest and Cornell, the latter an alumnus of Fairfield University and, like Forest, of the *Catholic Worker*, took over direction of the Fellowship. Berrigan remained close to it for some time.

From Prague, Berrigan proceeded on to the Soviet Union by invitation of the Orthodox and Baptist communities there. Once again the impact was mighty. "I was discovering for the first time, and at firsthand, the radically different social forms by which other decent men and women were living. I was discovering peaceable communities of faith, surviving and even thriving in most difficult and trying circumstances. I was seeing at firsthand the damage wrought to the human spirit in the West as a result of the Cold War."

It was no chastened Dan Berrigan who came back from that prescribed sabbatical in Europe. Quite the opposite. He had seen the United States and the escalating American military presence in Vietnam from new perspectives: the other side of the Atlantic, the other side of the Iron Curtain, the Christian Peace Conference. He was more than ever convinced that there was something sick about his native land. It was still two years before Dr. John C. Bennett, president of Union Theological Seminary, would make the startling assertion in *Christianity and Crisis* that United States involvement in Vietnam made it difficult for an American to be an American. But it was obvious that Berrigan was already of that frame of mind. He was convinced that the United States was about to repeat the bankrupt experience of the French in Indochina, with a new provocation and a new rhetoric. Thus, if he was a dissenter before on domestic social questions, it was as nothing to the dissention he would espouse on military issues. Further, like the conscientious fighter, he was honed physically for the match. Europe had transformed Berrigan in more ways than one. The flab was gone from the bones. "That chubby face of his had turned gaunt, yet incredibly serene," in Forest's words, "He had become ascetic, spiritual, unpriestly! It was a totally new vibration."

Indeed this was a totally new Berrigan, although still short of a fiercely independent one. He still sought imprimaturs for his books; he still put obedience to the rule before radical impulses of his own. Some superiors might have considered him a fearsome maverick, but in 1964 Dan Berrigan was yet something of a model, house-broken Jesuit.

—3—

Berrigan returned from Europe by way of Africa, his second extended trip to that continent. Back in New York he began a three-year stint as associate editor of *Jesuit Missions,* a polite monthly with a hefty circulation (158,376 at the time), but without the editorial clout of its sister publication across town, *America. Jesuit Missions* seemed about the last place in the world that anyone could get in hot water, but Berrigan managed to, quite quickly. First there was flak over his lifestyle. The breezy mode, the informal dress: turtleneck instead of Roman collar, ski jacket instead of overcoat—these sent shockwaves through the community on East 78th Street and the handsome brownstone that was once Emily Post's. A demon had returned to disturb the shades of ecclestiastical social etiquette. Word circulated of the poster-sized picture of Corita Kent, the artist (then Sister Mary Corita), decorating the walls of his shower; to her shoulder was pinned a button reading, "Save Water, Shower with a Friend." (The poster is gone now, but kindred whimsical posters have replaced it.) More disconcertingly, Berrigan joined in talk about adopting a child, a possibility that avant-garde priests were exploring at the time, partly out of protest against mandatory celibacy, partly out of their own love for children. Nothing came of that talk.

Meanwhile, once again there was great flak over Berrigan's liturgies: the indifference about vestments, the improvised Canons, the readings from contemporary writers and poets, the settings. Some of the liturgies were celebrated in his own apartment, some in the living rooms of friends, including a few of the exalted, for Berrigan by now was a vogue-ish creature, a controversialist, a prize-winning poet, an author, a lecturer, a "catch." Celebrate an exotic, off-beat liturgy in the living room, say, of Sargent Shriver—once head of the Peace Corps, future Ambassador to France, future vice-presidential nominee—and of course word is going to get back fast to headquarters, probably with some details embellished—although Dan Berrigan would be the first to admit that the reports of his doings even then needed little embellishing to be disturbing to many. It was not long before Berrigan was being told to "cool it." He did, to a degree. "If I am to be removed some day from the New York scene," he said to a friend, "it should be on a real issue, something having to do with the man in the ditch, rather than on the issue of liturgy."

The "real issue" turned out to be Vietnam. President Johnson had betrayed his campaign promises and escalated American intervention in Southeast Asia into a major war. Draft resisters were burning their Selective Service cards. Protesters were in the streets. Berrigan was there with them.

On October 16, 1965, David Miller, a young Catholic Worker, became the first to defy a new Federal law against the burning of draft cards, touching a cigarette lighter to his card before a gathering of 500 war protesters and media people outside the Whitehall Street Induction Center in lower Manhattan. Miller had been a student of Berrigan's at LeMoyne and a member of Berrigan's elite company of undergraduates. The association was not missed by the press. Indeed the connection was quickened across the country when Philip Berrigan gave a widely quoted interview with the Baltimore *Evening Sun* in which he termed Miller's act "the highest expression of loyalty" to his country.

Meanwhile back in New York Berrigan and two other prominent peace personalities, Rabbi Abraham Heschel of Conservative Judaism and Lutheran Pastor Richard Neuhaus from Brooklyn, were organizing a national ad hoc emergency committee named Clergy Concerned About Vietnam (now called simply Clergy and Laity Concerned). The purpose of the group was direct enough: war and peace were urgent concerns of all churches; thus, as concerned Vietnam, clergy were obliged in conscience to take the lead in opposing the one and promoting the other. It seemed a noble thought, a praiseworthy undertaking, certainly given the gospel messages; and the group did enroll as national committee members many of the nation's most prominent churchmen. They included Dr. Bennett, of Union Theological Seminary; the Rev. Eugene Carson Blake, secretary of the World Council of Churches; Dr. Martin Luther King, Dr. Robert McAfee Brown, Dr. Harvey Cox, Dr. William Sloane Coffin, Dr. Reinhold Niebuhr, Dr. Dana McLean Greeley. Catholic names were conspicuous by their absence, however, and this made Berrigan's listing as co-chairman of the group the more arresting. There was nervousness in peace circles. New York was hardly a congenial place then for an active priest-pacifist.

Cardinal Spellman was still around and his patriotic proclivities were known to one and all. The cardinal was making yet his annual Christmas trips to American troops around the world, and though he was not to say so in precise words until Christmas of 1966, it was apparent early on that he regarded Vietnam as "a war for civilization." The bishops of the United States were in step with him. In November, 1966 they issued their first joint statement on the war, weighing the principles of Vatican II and concluding that "it is reasonable to argue that our presence in Vietnam is justified." All this left Dan Berrigan in 1965 in an isolated wing of his church.

The issue came to a head with an incident that brought Spellman's chancellor, Archbishop John J. Maguire, flying home for Vatican II, clearly for the purpose of removing Berrigan from the activist scene and from the United States itself. It was November, 1965 and Roger LaPorte, 21, a Catholic Worker whom Berrigan knew through

Dorothy Day, immolated himself on the steps of the United Nations as a protest against the war. On his way to Bellevue Hospital Laporte exclaimed, "I am a Catholic Worker. I am antiwar, all wars. I did this as a religious act." The world kept a death vigil. Laporte died 30 hours later, and Berrigan was asked to deliver the eulogy at a service for him at the Worker. The eulogy was something of a sensation, for Berrigan refused to decry the immolation or brand Laporte's act a suicide. Suicide proceeds from despair and from the loss of hope, Berrigan maintained, and he did not feel that Laporte died in that spirit. Rather, said Berrigan, "his death was offered so that others may live."

Berrigan never recanted that point of view, although the viewpoint was to cause a great crisis in his life. "We had never known an occasion where a person freely offered his life, except on the field of battle or to save another person," Berrigan reflected later. "But the deliberate self-giving, a choice which didn't depend upon some immediate crisis but upon thoughtful revaluation of life— this was very new to us, and was, indeed, an unprecedented gift." In fact Berrigan came to regard Laporte's immolation of himself as something purer than the giving of one's life on a battlefield, and more in the tradition of Christ's own crucifixion.

"I think in Christianity that something very great has been lost," Berrigan said in the context of Laporte in his book *The Raft Is Not the Shore*. "Jesus' death, I think, in a very deep sense can be called a self-immolation. I mean that he went consciously to death, choosing that death for the sake of others, reasonably and thoughtfully. But the only way such a death continues in history as an example to others is in the military. Except for a few saints here and there who died for others; but that's very exceptional. In war, soldiers always go and die. And in many cases they die in religious wars. They die with the blessing: you will attain eternal life because you gave your life. But they die with weapons in their hands; they die at the hands of others with weapons. This seems to be contrary to the example of Jesus, who refused to take up the sword."

Within days of Laporte's immolation, rumors were speeding about linking the act to his friendship with Berrigan, rumors which Berrigan termed "atrocious." "It was not to be wondered," he added, "that a time of growing national madness was also infecting us, on our own scene." Between everything, church officials were goaded to act. Berrigan was removed by religious superiors as co-chairman of Clergy Concerned and packed off for Latin America on a hastily manufactured writing assignment for *Jesuit Missions*. He was to be gone indefinitely.

No one was admitting how far up the chain of command the order went, but it seemed clear from the timing of events. Maguire had returned carrying a directive from Spellman in Rome to Berrigan's Jesuit superiors; the man was to be gotten out of New York. Berrigan was never officially told this, and to this day that galls. "One of the great weaknesses, and the infection of secularity in the order," he says, "has been the secrecy. I have always thought that when Jesus said, 'I have always spoken openly,' and 'ask them what I have said,' that that is the way we are supposed to operate. Well anyway, when I was kicked out in '65 into Latin America, I never found out why. And they never said why. And to this day I don't know why. I have nothing but rumors and second-hand reports."

The dirty work was left to Father James Cotter, the editor of *Jesuit Missions*. Francine Gray recreates the ouster conversation in her book *Divine Disobedience:* Father Cotter walked into Berrigan's room at Jesuit Missions House and said:

"The fat's in the fire."

"I haven't got much fat, and where's the fire?" Berrigan responded.

"You've got to go on a trip," said Cotter.

"I don't feel much like traveling this winter," said Berrigan.

"You've got to go on a trip," Cotter repeated.

"What if I don't want to?" Berrigan asked.

"Be sensible," Cotter pleaded. "I've fought for you. It's infinitely better than what they'd originally planned for you," said Cotter, ominously.

"What was that?" Berrigan asked.

"I can't tell you," Cotter replied.

"The meat cleaver, huh?" Berrigan quipped.

The Laporte eulogy, Maguire's return from Rome, Cotter's dispatching of his junior editor—all this had taken place within the space of six days. Within another week, Berrigan was off for Mexico and nine other Latin American countries. Father Alden Stevenson, S.J., an Asian scholar and a photographer, joined Berrigan in Cuernavaca. They formed a team, Stevenson recording the sights of poverty and repression, Berrigan furnishing the words of moral outrage.

Like all of Berrigan's foreign experiences, the Latin American one helped radicalize him. He met Peace Corps people, Young Christian Workers, progressive bishops and the avant-garde of those clerics who gave inspiration to the Liberation Theology movement. This is the movement which would create a humane society through the refashioning of social, economic, and political structures which foster injustices, manifest, for example, in suppression of the poor and suppression in the name of economic and political law and order. It was indeed an exciting time to be in Latin America. The continent was in ferment; revolution was in the air. In Brazil, word reached Berrigan and Stevenson of the death of Camilo Torres. The young Colombian priest died while leading a guerrilla force against what he considered a corrupt landlord government in Bogota. Berrigan and Stevenson wondered whether justice could ever come to Latin America without widespread guerrilla actions and revolution.

Back in the United States, in the meantime, there was anger, bitter anger over the imperious dispatching of Berrigan to exile. In Manchester, New Hampshire a Catholic pacifist went on a hunger strike in St. Joseph's Cathedral to protest the action. Students at Notre Dame University began a fast, while in New York pickets marched outside Cardinal Spellman's residence on Madison Avenue, behind St. Patrick's Cathedral, carrying placards reading, "End Power Politics in the Church," and "Merry Christmas Dan Berrigan Wherever you Are." It was an unprecedented demonstration; Catholics didn't picket bishops in these days, much less cardinals. *Commonweal* decried the exiling as "a shame and a scandal, a disgustingly blind totalitarian act, a travesty on Vatican II," and a full-page advertisement appeared in the *New York Times* for December 12, 1965 protesting the exile and demanding Berrigan's return. It was placed by an ad hoc group called the Committee for Daniel Berrigan. Nearly one thousand persons signed the ad, more than 75 of them priests. The involvement of that many priests in an ecclesiastical protest was electrifying for the times.

Berrigan was kept abreast of much that was happening

back in the United States. Though some of the news was exhilarating, it did not keep him from slipping into moods of depression, particularly around Christmas time. His father wrote movingly, "Dear boy, I slept on thoughts of you and the true dimensions of your Greatness."

Such notes helped, but the note Berrigan seemed to be looking for especially—word from Merton—was slow in reaching him. It did not catch up to him until February, in Ecuador. When it came, it was, as Berrigan himself described it, a lifeline. This was the note in which Merton declined to feel sorry for Berrigan's having to go to Latin America, and in which he said Latin America was where "everything is going to happen." Additional advice from Merton admonished Berrigan on concepts of authority and obedience, and wound up saying, "let us work for the church and for people, not for ideas and programs." It was the perfect letter for a critical moment. It gave Berrigan a renewed grip on his Jesuitism, and set the tone for his reentry into the activist scene in the United States. At a press conference at the Biltmore Hotel in New York after Berrigan's return, Cotter stuck fast to the official line that Berrigan's had been a routine assignment. He denied that Berrigan had been silenced for his protests against the Vietnam war, and he said that he was free to resume his peace activities immediately. A certain credulousness was demanded for some of the comments, but Berrigan supporters were in a position to be generous. Their hero was back and he would resume the position of co-chairman of Clergy Concerned. Further, Berrigan supporters had demonstrated that effective protest was indeed possible within the church. Let the official line say what it may, the fact was that high-ranking churchmen had backed away under pressure from a decision that hitherto would have been as permanent as cement. A new day had come to American Catholicism.

Berrigan's provincial during this time of testing, and therefore the person responsible on paper for Berrigan's reassignment, was Father James McGinty, S.J. He died of cancer several years ago, officially silent still about background details of the exile.

"We never had any contact after he left office," Berrigan commented, "and I suddenly heard that he was terminally ill. So I wrote him a letter in the hospital. I didn't want to just go over and visit, because I thought maybe that would be just too shocking for a dying person. But I wrote him, and I said that, you know, there was reconciliation in the air and I hoped we could be friends, and that I was keeping him in my prayers. Well, he was too weak to answer, but he sent a message back about how much that meant to him. When I heard that, I went and saw him—only a few days before he died. The meeting was quick and quiet. We shook hands. We didn't say very much—he was terribly weak; he died only two or three days later. It was more the gesture than the words that was important. That was the best I could do. But I never got the facts of the case."

—4—

Returned to the domestic peace scene, Berrigan was immediately at the center of the action. Public protests were mushrooming against the war, and Berrigan could be spotted up front—but not forever. Together with his brother Phil, he gradually became convinced that the standard type of protest was innocuous, "another liberal bag," polite, nicely fashionable, and tolerated by the establishment to the point of ineffectiveness on the part of the protestors. Thus both Berrigans were to bow out, including out of Clergy Concerned and the Catholic Peace Fellowship. Each in his own way was coming to the conclusion that a new community of risk, a new level of dissent was necessary if the witness for peace was really to have impact on the waging of the war.

At this point, Dan Berrigan was obviously still groping. Phil, now stationed at St. Peter Claver parish in Baltimore and immersed in a variety of social issues, seemed more sure of the direction he should go. He had become extremely contemptuous of "educational outreach" and dialectic. He had attempted persuasion on Maryland's senators, with whom he had met in their offices; he had debated a Maryland congressman; he had sat down for a two-hours' exchange with then Secretary of State Dean Rusk. When it was obvious nothing of substance would result, he gave up on talk. He moved to a series of demonstrations at Fort Meyers, Virginia, three in fact, demonstrations that became increasingly spectacular and raucous—the Provost Marshal of the fort heaping "sons of bitches" and other epithets on Phil and his colleagues. Phil was disconcerted to find the demonstrations did not bring about the arrest and court appearance which he courted for personal as well as propaganda reasons. He had long since come to the conclusion that in time of war a priest is obliged to do something that gets him locked up; he could not just play the game. It developed that Dan would actually be the first of the brothers to be arrested and land in jail. This is surprising since at the time he was not clear in his mind about what action to adopt to move witness to a new level of dissent.

That his brother Phil should have been out front in perceptions of a new witness does not in retrospect surprise Dan. There was a time when the youngest of the six Berrigan brothers looked to the next up the line for his leads on life, but this had ended. "I think in the very early phase of our priesthood, and even in the seminary, that I was a big, strong leader to him," says Dan of Phil. "I helped him get started on some things, because his own community wasn't really offering him the kind of outlets that would urge him on. It was a pretty dead crowd. But his talents and his understanding grew so quickly once he got a little bit of foothold. I remember quite vividly saying to myself by the time I came back from Europe in '64 that this business of Phil following my lead is all over. It was quite clear that he was setting his own pace and going in his own direction."

This is not to suggest that while Phil was moving to dramatic protest—guerrilla theater, if you will—Dan was treading water. It is only to say that Dan Berrigan was still preoccupied with the ecclesiastical scene—for instance, scoring the American bishops for their lack of moral leadership on the war and struggling within his own order for a quickened sensibility with respect to the fighting and bombing and dying. Two incidents in those days particularly disturbed tranquillity within the Jesuit community.

In 1967, Dan Berrigan was invited through the Fellowship of Reconciliation and some Quaker friends to be part of a group that would go to Hanoi with medical supplies. The shipment was to be largely a symbolic one. It would call attention to the American embargo on medical supplies to North Vietnam, and it would point up the desperate need for medical help because of the incessant bombing of the country by American planes. Although the mission had political overtones, Berrigan viewed it as essentially humanitarian. He approached his provincial and carefully laid out the proposal that he join in the mission. "All hell broke loose," he says. Berrigan recalls the incident involving the provincial:

"He said, 'Under no circumstances. The answer is a flat no. It was not to be done,' et cetera, et cetera. I said it was going to be done. I said my conscience at that point was adamant, and I was going. Well, he said, when there is this kind of impasse the general (of the Jesuit order) allows a litigation, and we can agree on four priests and sit down with the problem. I said fine. So we had this big thing at Kohlman Hall at Fordham. I laid out papers and explained the issue. I still was sort of zonked as to why all this fracas over a simple matter of compassion. Everyone took the thing very solemnly. At one point, a question like this arose—and I bring this up because it was symptomatic of those times and the vise in which people were locked over what I took to be small potatoes—one of them said, 'Would you consider that you had committed a mortal sin if you did not go?' And I looked him straight in the face and said, 'I don't like to put it that way, but if you want to, yes.' Well at the end of this the four of them said, 'We don't see any great objection.' Obviously this was a great blow to the provincial. He had expected to be able to get me through these four. He rose up like a jack-in-the-box and said, 'I have some other questions here.' I rose up like a jack-in-the-box and said, 'There will be no other questions here. I'm walking out. We have finished the question we came for.' And I walked out."

In a way, it was all academic, because the plan to ship the medical supplies fell through. In another sense, however, the exercise at Kohlman Hall was far from academic, as it hardened Berrigan's attitude toward authority—or at least what he considered its unfair application.

Three or four months later came another invitation to

go to Hanoi, this time with activist professor Howard Zinn of Boston University as a representative of a coalition of peace groups to secure the release of three captured American fliers. "At that point," says Berrigan, "I had had it with the authorities. I went, and I sent them a registered letter saying I had gone."

It was a chancy action to have taken, certainly so far as his remaining a Jesuit was concerned. There were several times during those years when Berrigan's dismissal from the order was under active consideration. Aware that this was one such time, Berrigan once again turned to Merton for counsel and advice. "The one real thought I have is that obviously sooner or later it is going to be a question of obeying God or obeying man," Merton wrote back, April 15, 1967. "Is the issue as clear as you put it? Are they throwing you out if you go to North Vietnam without approval? Is it clear to everyone? Should you simply make this known and see what happens? In other words, is the best, clearest, simplest, cleanest thing just to go to North Vietnam and let them do the terrible and dirty thing they want to do? I feel very sorry for these people."

The "terrible and dirty thing" never happened. Sensing that Berrigan's dismissal would trigger disruptions within the order, authorities turned discreet. His dossier was transferred to the provincial for universities, and Berrigan reported back to him. "He gave me a minor slap on the wrist when I came in," Berrigan comments, "and said something like, 'Well, you, know, if you had really laid this out before us, we would have allowed you to go.' I said, 'No, that was not the point.'"

As for the trip to Hanoi, it was both success and exasperating disappointment. Berrigan and Zinn exited North Vietnam with the American pilots, but they were unable to get them to return with them by commercial carrier to the

United States. This was a matter Berrigan and Zinn considered of vital importance. It was urgent, they felt, that through to its completion the trip be a symbol of an independent peace action, taken at the initiative of North Vietnam and responded to by Americans who were resisting the war in their own country. Moreover, the Vietnamese had explicitly connected the integrity of the trip, and its visibility as a peace gesture, to the fate of other American prisoners in North Vietnam and the possibility of future releases. Berrigan and Zinn thought they had convinced the prisoners of the advisability of their returning to the United States with them. But this was not to be. The release plane touched down in Vientiane, and there the fliers were gathered under the wing of the American Ambassador to Laos, William Sullivan, and a bevy of military officials. There was minimal courtesy, no thanks to Berrigan and Zinn for their efforts—or even for the risk they had run. And there had been great risk, for the American bombing of North Vietnam continued all the while they were there. In fact, several times both Berrigan and Zinn were forced to take shelter in bunkers from American bombers. Berrigan recorded one such moment in a moving poem. . . .

> I picked up the littlest
> a boy, his face
> breaded with rice (his sister calmly feeding him
> as we climbed down)
>
> In my arms fathered
> in a moment's grace, the messiah
> of all my tears. I bore, reborn
>
> a Hiroshima child from hell.

The poem appears in the diary of the trip which Berrigan published under the title *Night Flight to Hanoi.*

If Berrigan felt let down by the American dimensions of the experience, it was understandable. It was not just his own government and the military who were ungrateful, but seemingly the fliers as well. Further, there was betrayal, when at least one of the fliers went back on his word. "They made a promise as the condition of their release—which I thought was a very minimal condition— that they would have nothing to do with the future bombing of North Vietnam, once they got back to their country," says Berrigan. "One of them was a major or colonel. I read years later that he was teaching at an Air Force base in Florida—teaching those who were going into bombing during the war. So he broke his promise."

"But one would have expected that," Berrigan adds with some bitterness.

There was even minimal gratitude expressed by the families of the fliers, although the fault may not have been entirely theirs. "The only messages I ever got from the families of the fliers were calls after midnight or in the early morning—very frightened people with great tremors about their having been instructed not to get in touch with us. This happened several times, so I'm sure the lid was put on those people," says Berrigan.

Shortly before Christmas of 1972, Berrigan read in the *New York Times* about one of the fliers he and Zinn had brought out of North Vietnam. The story—which mentioned neither Berrigan nor Zinn nor the full circumstances involving the flier's release—told of the terrible time he was having adjusting to life, after having been so long in solitary in North Vietnam. The former flier could not stand being alone in his house; he found it very disturbing to go outdoors in crowds. "I was very touched by this," says Berrigan, "because he was, above all, the one who showed some humanity toward us, and put up some objection to the ambassador's stealing the three of them away in the airplane there in Vientiane. So I sat down and wrote him a letter. I said that I had been through a few things too since we met. There are jails here and there are jails there, and I said I just wanted to wish you a good Christmas with your family and hope that things improve for you. So of course I never heard from him."

—5—

In August of 1967, Berrigan was invited to become associate director of United Religious Work at Cornell University in Ithaca, the first Catholic priest ever to be so asked. He said yes, but with some initial qualms. "I left New York with trepidation and many second thoughts," he says. "It appeared to me a choice of utmost seriousness, to decide to leave the peace community, which was in perennial need of all kinds. But I decided to go because Cornell was a new scene to me, and because the university had changed so rapidly in the previous two years. I must say that I have never had a serious regret for the choice I then made."

Cornell, in fact, turned out to be one of the most stimulating experiences of his life as a priest. The post gave him a measure of independence that he obviously craved. For the first time he was truly out from under the wing of the order. He was much his own man, with his own life to lead, in surroundings at last which he found intellectually congenial and temperamentally challenging. Cornell prided itself on a history of liberalism, so Berrigan was no maverick here. His associates included a priest and a minister who had burned their draft cards; the student body had large contingents of liberals and radicals, including strong SDS and black-liberation elements. The latter kept his concern for civil rights and justice for black people simulated, and he ranged on campus and off in support of causes of blacks.

This support was unqualified. He traveled to Boston, for example, to attend a meeting in a Catholic church in the city's South End called in order to raise money for a Black Panther defense fund. John Cort, a former Catholic Worker, labor organizer, and Peace Corps official, approached Berrigan at a reception afterward at the Jesuits' Warwick House to express some reservations about the Panthers. He did not consider his opinions presumptuous, much less racist. After all, he lived with a wife and nine children in a black ghetto, and only a hundred yards from a Panthers' headquarters. Cort was appalled by the tactics used by police to harass, hound, and in some places to shoot down Panthers. On the other hand, the Panthers had declared a kind of open warfare on police and the whole democratic system, and whatever the faults of both, Cort was not ready to go that far. He sought to convey something of this to Berrigan. Berrigan cut him off with the comment, "That's a typical white man's reaction."

At Cornell, Berrigan was in his milieu, and he relished it. Within a month of arrival he was taking a public position in support of a student who had ripped up his draft card and was facing trial. In another month he was taking a group of Cornell students to Washington for a massive march on the Pentagon. The demonstration proved fateful for Berrigan, for when the time permits expired, he joined those who refused to leave. The march had become a sit-in. Around midnight he was gathered up by police and put in jail. This was October 21, 1967. Berrigan refused bail and, Gandhi-like, went on a fast.

This was Berrigan's first arrest, his first time in jail—for him or any other Berrigan for that matter. There was no sense of shame, no feeling of disgrace. Quite the contrary. There was satisfaction and pride. "For the first time," he wrote in his diary, "I put on the prison blue jeans and denim shirt; a clerical attire I highly recommend for a new church. . . ."

A week later Berrigan was released. A priest-friend picked him up. They were crossing town with the car radio on when a news broadcast announced that four persons had just been arrested for pouring blood into the files of Selective Service offices at the United States Customs House in Baltimore. One of the four was Father Philip Berrigan, S.S.J. The date was October 27, 1967. Dan wrote in his diary: "This is the day of Phil's action in Baltimore. *Oremus pro fratribus in periculo.* 'Give honor to the Lord of Hosts, to him only. Let him be your only fear, let him be your only dread.'" (Isaiah 8:13)

Phil Berrigan's associates on the blood-pouring foray were Thomas Lewis, an artist and teacher, a Catholic; James Mengel, a former Army chaplain and a minister of the United Church of Christ; and David Eberhardt, son of a Presbyterian minister but himself an agnostic. The idea of the raid was conceived in Baltimore and involved Baltimore people. At the moment there was no urgency to reach out further. Dan knew the raid was coming, but was not asked to be a part of it.

It was different, however, when Phil—free on bail while awaiting sentencing for defacing government property—came up with the idea for the Catonsville action. This was to be a radical escalation of witness. It would be more ambitious, more complicated, more dangerous, and possibly of far-reaching consequences. It would require more people, and it would require people of a special dedication and commitment. Dan was approached.

"We had a lot of exchanges by letter," Dan reflects back. "Phil was going much deeper into resistance, and I was around this level of draft counseling, seeing my business at Cornell as being the advocate of young people who were going through their crisis of induction—or *un*duction. We were exchanging letters on this whole thing, and he was very helpful in my sorting out matters. He would say things like, 'We've got to find ways of translating the consciousness of young people into people our age.' He criticized the Benjamin Spock and Robert Sloane Coffin trial.

"Spock and Coffin and two others were on trial in Boston for conspiracy against the United States government in counseling and abetting young men to resist the draft. Phil saw them as being people who sort of reacted to the government, instead of initiating action. Phil didn't find that very exciting. He also found their defense at the trial just vapid, not interesting, not powerful, and not clear. Well, all those things were churning in my mind. Then he confronted me very strongly on this business of counseling others to go do things, when we should be stepping out ourselves. So he was working on me, and I was trying to be very thoughtful about what I would do.

"Well, by this time he was out on bail and was running around the country talking again. It was quite clear that he was not going to stop with that early action of the Baltimore Four. He and Lewis were both determined to act again, and they were around talking and recruiting people. Anyway, they came to Cornell—this would be in early spring, around March. We stayed up all one night, and Phil said this is what we're going to do. We have about nine or ten people, and how about it? Of course I was much more inclined to take that thing much more seriously. I told him I wanted 24 hours to think it over. I think I'll be with it, I said, but I really want to try my moods a little more. And if you don't hear from me in 24 hours, I'm in. I went out alone, and I prayed, and I meditated and thought about it. It all made sense."

The rest is resistance history.

At 12:30 p.m. on May 17, 1968, seven men and two women entered the Knights of Columbus Building in Catonsville, an all-white, middle-class suburb of Baltimore. They climbed the stairs to Selective Service offices on the second floor, burst in, emptied 1-A files from several cabinets into three wire trash baskets, and hurried them out to the parking lot. There they doused them with homemade napalm—made, to officialdom's subsequent embarrassment, from instructions provided by a military manual. They applied matches, blessed themselves, and in unison recited the Our Father, as they awaited their fate—or destiny, as the case may be. Cameras whirred and clicked. Pencils scribbled. For the media had been alerted that something momentous would be happening around noontime. Meanwhile, a statement was being distributed outlining the rationale of the raiders:

"Today, May 17th, we enter Local Board No. 33 at Catonsville, Maryland to seize Selective Service records and burn them with napalm manufactured by ourselves from a recipe in the Special Forces Handbook, published by the U.S. Government. We, American citizens, have worked with the poor in the ghetto and abroad. We destroy these draft records not only because they exploit our young men, but because they represent misplaced power concentrated in the ruling class of America. . . . We confront the Catholic church, other Christian bodies and synagogues of America with their silence and cowardice in the face of our country's crimes. We are convinced that the religious bureaucracy in this country is racist, is an accomplice in war, and is hostile to the poor. . . . Now this injustice must be faced, and this we intend to do, with whatever strength of mind, body, and grace that God will give us. May God have mercy on our nation."

The raid was a tactical success perhaps beyond the very dreams of the raiders. The exercise took only 90 seconds and went off with the precision—if one is allowed to make the analogy—of a military operation. In addition to the Berrigan brothers and Lewis, the raiders included David Darst, a Christian Brother; Thomas Melville, a former Maryknoll priest in Latin America; his wife, Marjorie Melville, a former Maryknoll nun, also in Latin America; George Mische, a former State Department employee; Mary Moylan, a registered nurse; and John Hogan, a former Maryknoll brother. Unlike the Baltimore Four, this was an all-Catholic cast, and that detail was to prove decisive in inspiring an American Catholic left to organize and contest U.S. involvement in Vietnam.

The nine entered the draft offices and went briskly about their business—the men requisitioning the draft records (they got 378 in all); the women restraining the clerks, all women. Their restraint mainly involved reaching over shoulders and keeping the buttons of phones down. One clerk managed to pitch a phone through a closed window in an attempt to attract attention. Another grabbed one of the wire baskets suddenly filled with draft files, and suffered a cut on the forefinger when it was pulled free. The cut was not a serious one. It required a bandaid, not stitches. More traumatic to the women clerks was the shock of what was taking place. Priests in clerical attire, men and women in neat, clean street clothes were doing violence to government records—this did not happen in America. What had the world come to? They were puzzled, dazed, shaken.

Outside the police were quickly on the scene, asking questions, politely addressing the Fathers as "Father," and, like the women upstairs, no doubt wondering what in the world things had come to when priests and ostensibly respectable citizens engaged in actions such as this. Dan Berrigan had a response for such wonderment in the mails. Just a few hours before the match was set to the napalm in Catonsville, he mailed to his publisher the manuscript for *Night Flight to Hanoi.* Its foreword anticipated the day's events and contained a passage that was to become manifesto for the Catonsville Nine and ultimately charter for the American Catholic left:

"Our apologies, good friends, for the fracture of good order, the burning of paper instead of children, the angering of the orderlies in the front parlor of the charnel house. We could not, so help us God, do otherwise. For we are sick at heart; our hearts give us no rest for thinking of the Land of Burning Children. And for thinking of that other Child, of whom the poet Luke speaks. The infant was taken up in the arms of an old man, whose tongue grew resonant and vatic at the touch of that beauty. And the old man spoke: this child is set for the fall and rise of many in Israel, a sign that is spoken against.

"Small consolation; a child born to make trouble, and to die for it, the first Jew (not the last) to be subject of a 'definitive solution.' He sets up the cross and dies on it; in the Rose Garden of the executive mansion, on the D.C. Mall, in the courtyard of the Pentagon. We see the sign, we read the direction; you must bear with us, for his sake. Or if you will not, the consequences are our own."

Within 15 minutes all nine were in custody and hustled off to Baltimore County Jail to face charges of conspiracy and destruction of government property. For Dan, the count was four felonies and two misdemeanors.

Next day, to assuage hurt and shock among the draft-board clerks, the raiders arranged from jail for flowers to be sent around to the women. "All of us sent them," says Phil Berrigan, "but of course it was Dan's idea. He's really wonderful about these fine human touches, these acts of consideration, if you will."

But not everyone was assuaged. Some weeks later, Phil received a letter from the daughter of the woman who had received the cut to her finger. "It was after we had been sentenced for the Customs House action, and Lewis and myself had gotten six years. We were in Towson County Jail. Rather than sending us up to Pennsylvania to the federal pen, they were holding us there for subsequent court actions. Anyway I received this letter from her. She had been a Vista worker, and I had worked pretty intimately with Vista over in West Baltimore, so I guess she had heard of me indirectly. She was outraged about her mother being hurt, and outraged over the kind of psychological and spiritual wedge that had been driven into that family by Catonsville."

—6—

In point of fact, many wedges were driven in many different directions by the action in Catonsville, including into the Catholic peace community itself. Dorothy Day, though obviously concerned about the danger involved in the destruction of property, spoke of Catonsville as an act of liturgy. "It's an act of prayer," she remarked to the Liturgical Conference in Washington. "It's an extension of the Eucharist." Few were so gracious. Many dismissed the action as the work of "kooks" or "romantics," people possessed of an egomania, a terrible naiveté, a weird evangelism, a psychotic sense of guilt—take your pick. The Catholic press was disapproving or dumb-struck. For instance, liberal *Commonweal*: Two years hence it would say of the Berrigan brothers as titular leaders of the American Catholic left that they were "exceptional individuals with a sense of humanity, irony, and modesty about what they are doing which distinguishes them not only from many others who claim the title 'revolutionary' but also from most of the 'commonsensical' men who rule us." But at this juncture, it trod as if on eggs. It was supportive on its "News and Views" page, one person's opinion, but silent in its editorial columns, except to say of Philip Berrigan in the context of his sentencing for blood-pouring in Baltimore that he acted out of a tradition that "has always made room for the legitimate, violent revolt." There was no allusion to Catonsville. Even Merton, the old loyalist, was perplexed. Catonsville, he wrote in the magazine *Ave Maria*, was an "attempt at prophetic nonviolent provocation, but it bordered on violence and was violent to the extent that it meant pushing some good ladies around and destroying some government property."

Merton feared that the peace movement was escalating beyond peaceful protest—in which case, he said, "It may also be escalating into self-contradiction." He concluded that Catonsville "frightened more than it edified." Not even violence-prone activists were persuaded about the effectiveness of actions such as that at Baltimore and Catonsville. For them, it was all too symbolic and ultimately meaningless. With data banks and computers, for instance, could not the records destroyed at Catonsville be reconstructed in a matter of days? One radical dismissed them as "lollipop revolutionaries."

For the Catonsville participants, little of this was to the point. They saw themselves in a gospel tradition. Hadn't Jesus himself exploded at the money-changers and thrown them out of the temple? They saw themselves as part of an old Catholic story—people of conscience daring to stand against the state in a witness for life and truth: Joan of Arc, Thomas More, the protesting Jesuits of Hitler's Germany. These people gave their lives; they would give, if not life itself, then years of life behind bars.

Critics labeled this presumptuous, and a few called them sanctimonious moral itches. Many old friends turned them off, and this opened wounds, some of which have never healed. On the other hand, many—particularly young people—were attracted to this unique type of witness, and within weeks resistance communities were springing up in Milwaukee, Washington, New York, Chicago, Rochester, and Camden. The composition of these communities was overwhelmingly Catholic, partly because of the example of the Berrigan brothers, and partly because the witness stressed emphasis on liturgy and the Eucharist. When supporters were being rallied to come to Baltimore in early October for the opening of the Catonsville Nine trial, for instance, they were urged not to go first to the Court House or the courtroom, but to assemble at St. Ignatius Church for a worship service for peace. Whatever the underlying reasons for its attraction, it was apparent that, as evolving, the activist peace community was as Catholic as a parochial school. By April, 1969, 36 activists were free on bail for Catonsville-type actions. Author Charles Meconis calculated that all but six of them were Catholics. Twenty-one of the 31 men were past or present priests; three of the five women were past or present nuns.

As the movement made its shift from marches and sit-ins to the symbolic destruction of property deemed to be serving perverse ends, sizable "communities of resistance" built up about the actions in the drama, involving hundreds, indeed thousands of people who were not themselves aggressive political activists.

Dan Berrigan explains the phenomenon: "Some of the political activists said that a moral, individual action was no longer enough. There must be unity of effort which was more and more highly political. One person refusing induction or going on trial or leaving the university would have no impact. Now there must be community behind him or her. Resistance, of course, was as ambiguous as the people who engaged in it. Some saw it as a violent word, some as nonviolent. I never heard the phrase 'communities of resistance,' as such, until around 1970; the word *resistance* around 1967 or 1968. But the idea evolved that there should be communities, each member of which was dedicated to some violent or nonviolent ideal, some political or spiritual ideal, or some combination of these—political and spiritual. I think it just to say that the roots of all this were among the religious people. I think they saw it first. Actually around that time, mainly as a result of Catonsville and the draft-board actions, people began to say that it was not enough to perform one action and disperse. People had to stay together preparing for trial, talking around the country, preparing legal defense, raising money, educating other people."

Which is precisely what happened, ultimately in a very

major way. There was one astonishing effect of this development. That was the inability of these communities of resistance to hold as Catholics very many persons whose impulses for involvement arose in the first place out of their very Catholicism. A disconcertingly large number drifted off into a variety of secularist ideologies or into nothingness, contemptuous of the faith and some even of the religious convictions that had virtually inspired them to act. Meconis notes the phenomenon in his book *With Clumsy Grace*, although he pursues it only sketchily.

Dan Berrigan is aware of the phenomenon also, and addressed it with me in the limited context of his fellow Jesuits and the community which grouped in the common rooms of the building on 98th Street on New York's upper west side. This is the same building in which Berrigan lives today, along with other survivors of the Woodstock-Union Theological Seminary experiment, the attempt at joint ecumenical theological training that the Jesuits jettisoned in 1973.

During the Vietnam years, the building on 98th Street was electric with activity. "Meetings of some of the most courageous antiwar Jesuits and their friends took place in this building," recounts Berrigan. "A lot of civil disobedience was planned here, and the building was under FBI surveillance. The place became notorious in a good and a bad way, as it turned out. I knew that history only by hearsay. People went to jail from here, and went to the courts from here. Women were living here with men, and the dining room was free and easy. There was a spirit I take to be a very exciting one. But it was also a very chaotic one."

The West Side Jesuit community was large then, numbering perhaps as many as 150 men, most of them scholastics 30-ish in age. Some are gone now from Catholicism, and so are many of their closest co-activists, male and female. Is there an inherent weakness in institutional Catholicism that it should not be able to hold so many of the best and the brightest, so many of the most motivated Catholics?

Berrigan rejects that notion. "None of these people was really institutionalized," he says. "The brand of Catholicism that they brought to their actions out of their immediate past was not institutional either. Most of them had found a new way of faith before these actions. The quandary is an even deeper one, because it wasn't really a question of separating from the institution. It was a question of wiping out the whole thing, faith as such. And that's what I find a source of great sorrow."

"It's hard to figure it all out," he continues. "The ones I knew best, of course, were the Jesuits—and I have to speak tentatively, because I don't want to be harsh. I felt that people didn't keep up a discipline in the community life and the connections with friends that would have resulted in something better. Then, even while rejecting America, they took to aspects of America that were very, very questionable, and kind of drowned out there. Because I'm not convinced that in leaving they found anything better. It is one question to leave, but the point is, where are you going to arrive? What have you found that is morally or humanly superior to what you left? I think people didn't ask that. I must say that over the years I haven't seen much better anywhere than what I have been trying to hang onto."

On the spiritual level, Berrigan is convinced that "there was a loss of a sense of prayer, a loss of the sacraments, a loss of the Eucharist." After a while he began to say to himself, "I don't belong in that direction. I don't belong with these people anymore."

"You can talk to others in this community about their conduct around here, the way they segregated themselves at meals, and the way in which they brought in their own friends and sat with them in their own groups—week after week, month after month—and showed a kind of contempt for people in the order here. Well, I found I couldn't go that way and didn't want to. And so it went."

The drainage to Catholicism in the communities of resistance was especially pronounced among women, and Berrigan attributes that in considerable degree to the very rude awakening of many of them to "sexism" within the movement. "Women began to feel that they had their own struggle, that the church was unsympathetic, and that even the clerics involved in the movement were not on their side or were not understanding. So, many of them walked out. It goes on like that. And part of it was our fault."

In fact, says Berrigan, the fault is everywhere. "Part of it is the fault of the Jesuit superiors, who during those years were, I think, notably resistant to that kind of peace activity and made it much more difficult for these young Jesuits by threatening them with eviction or with not being ordained, thus casting a pall over this whole scene. There was a very angry response and a growing breach for years. One can only think, what if only all sides had been a little bit more human and flexible, and if superiors had not laid out manifestos about obedience—and if, on the other hand, the peace community had been more peaceable and more of a community?"

—7—

The Catonsville trial was both brief and long. The defendants would have been satisfied with a single day in court; they got four, from October 5–9, 1968. They used the time strategically.

"We realized, before we entered into social jeopardy, that there would be no opportunity for an open plea before the court," says Berrigan. "So we entered on the trial with different ambitions, a different vocabulary, and even, I dare say, different spiritual resources. In principle, the courts, up to the United States Supreme Court itself, are unwilling, especially in wartime, to consider seriously the moral and legal questions of war itself. So we felt that civilized men must speak in the courtroom in order to achieve some public audibility about who we were and what we were about. The issues raised by the war—issues of the constitutionality and morality of the war, of free speech and freedom of protest—might thereby be separated from our personal or corporate fates. We were obliged in fact to attain some kind of personal liberation before acting at all, a certain spiritual detachment from the fact of prison. So, in a sense, the scenario of the trial was written before the action itself occurred."

From the outset, the defendants sought to identify themselves with those in the streets and the ghettos, with those who face the draft, prison, war, or exile, with the poor and the powerless—indeed, says Berrigan satirically, with those at the outer end of America's "merciful" activity in economics, politics, militarism, and diplomacy throughout the world. "We tried to achieve clarity about our faith," Berrigan explains, "to manifest a visible unity between the events in the courtroom and those who had gathered by the thousands in the city to support us, and, by implication, between ourselves and the larger world of victims created by the war."

"We told our stories as simply and directly as we could,"

Berrigan reflected later. "We related how, from many different points of the compass, from different ages, different traditions, we had converged upon one judgment. If the war were total, the peace also must be total in its claim upon the person. No longer could we place upon a certain group the burden of our original sin—the oldest sin of history, constantly reinvigorated, restated as original for each generation by the forging of a new language of hatred, division, and death."

The trial was orderly. The judge—Roszel Thomsen, 66, Chief Federal Judge, Fourth Federal District—gave his charge to the jury. Then, while the jury deliberated, he invited the defendants to speak in open court about their impression of the trial, the issues, and the reception which they had received. The result was an exchange extraordinary within anyone's memory in that courtroom. "For some 90 minutes," says Berrigan, "we engaged in a very heated, intense, and, at times, profound exchange with this old man, shaken by the rigorous days he had undergone in a case of great complexity, and fought with passion on both sides."

The exchange did not figure in the outcome of the trial, of course. It did, however, furnish some select material for the 1970 verse play which Berrigan constructed from the transcript of the trial, *The Trial of the Catonsville Nine*. The play was a sensational success. It opened in Hollywood, went into repertory, and came to New York. The play won the Los Angeles Drama Critics Circle Award for 1971 and the *Village Voice's* off-Broadway "Obie" for the same year. It was translated into several languages, its messages thus leaping oceans to Japan, France, Greece. It was, in Berrigan bibliographer Anne Klejment's opinion, Berrigan's "most influential and most powerful statement against the war." As a book, the play went into several printings, as well as into Beacon and Bantam paperback editions. Then the publishers allowed it go out of print. Berrigan, ordinarily not given to vulgarisms, says that "really pisses me off. Teachers are still using that play in courses on campus—it's about the war years, you know. And I find it awful that the publisher would let it go out of print."

The verdict at Catonsville was as expected. The defendants were found guilty on each of three counts: destruction of United States property, destruction of Selective Service records, and interference with the Selective Service Act of 1967. Four weeks later they were sentenced. Darst, Moylan, Marjorie Melville, and Hogan received two-year terms; Daniel Berrigan, Thomas Melville, and Mische, three years; Philip Berrigan and Lewis, three-and-a-half years, to run concurrently with the six-years' sentences they received for the blood-pouring in Baltimore. (Darst, the youngest of the Catonsville Nine, was fated not to serve his sentence. He died tragically in an automobile accident October 20, 1969, en route to a peace rally.) Seven of the nine were freed that day, pending appeal. Philip Berrigan and Lewis were remanded to jail, and would have to wait six weeks for bail. The appeals' process was unsuccessful. The U.S. Court of Appeals upheld the convictions, though it sent the cases of four—one being Phil Berrigan's—back to the trial judge to reconsider the severity of the sentences. The Supreme Court refused to review the convictions.

The drama was far from ended, however. Instead of surrendering to federal authorities in April, as directed, several of the convicted elected to go underground as "fugitives for peace," including the two Berrigans. Phil's caper ended quickly; he was picked up after ten days, plucked from a closet of St. Gregory the Great rectory in upper Manhattan. Dan's trip underground lasted four months, and was spectacular both in its innocence and its professionalism.

His descent into the underground was largely an unplanned thing. Initially it seemed to involve merely overstaying his surrender date and staying out of sight for a couple of weeks in order to take part in a festival at Cornell that would bring together some 10,000 students in a post-Woodstock happening of art, politics, communal living, all in honor of nonviolence, Catonsville and, of course, Berrigan himself. At 7:40 p.m. on Friday, April 17, Berrigan ended ten rustic days in hiding on the land and entered Cornell's great Barton Hall in spectacular fashion. In his own words, he was decked out "gorgeously—like an outer-space insect, in big goggles, motorcycle helmet and jacket, surrounded by a troupe of students, variously hirsute, hippy, fierce, and celebrational." He roared in on the back of a motorcycle, and when he walked on the stage, there was pandemonium. The FBI waited in the wings, frozen by the throng and the excitement. To have moved then on Berrigan would have been to incite a riot.

The next hour-and-a-half were stormy, indeed. Says Berrigan: "I recall a sense of weightlessness, almost of dislocation; the throng of young faces, singing, dancing, eating, the calls of support and resistance. Much love, many embraces, the usual press of journalists. Then, in a quiet moment, a friend whispered: 'Do you want to split?' "

It was all Berrigan needed. As he was to write, "Why not indeed split? Why concede, by hanging around, that wrong-headed power owned me? Why play mouse, even sacred mouse, to their cat game? Why turn this scene into yet another sanctuary, so often done before, only delaying the inevitable, the hunters always walking off with their prize?"

In a flash his mind was made up. When the lights lowered for a rock group, he slipped off back stage. Students lowered around him an enormous puppet of one of the twelve Apostles, in use shortly before by a mime group. Inside the burlap, Berrigan had only to hold a stick that kept the papier-maché head aloft, and follow the others, making for a panel truck in which the costumes were to be packed. The puppets were pitched aboard. Berrigan climbed in—blind as a bat, he said, sure of his radar, spoiling for fun. "It was guerrilla theater, a delight, just short of slapstick." A FBI agent spotted the escape. The license plate number was recorded. The chase was on that was to last four months.

Later, Berrigan was asked which papier-maché apostle had he slipped inside of. He responded in good humor that he never knew. "I just had hopes that it wasn't Judas," he said. "I wouldn't mind any of the others—if they wouldn't."

When Berrigan went underground, the truest of believers were hard put to see the action as much more than a gesture of defiance which would only prejudice his chances for reduction of sentence and early parole. Certainly few saw the act as contributing significantly to the peace movement or marking a new development in the moral revolution of which he had become the symbolic leader. Most expected that the FBI would quickly lay hands on him, as it had on Phil. It didn't turn out that way. The FBI combed Berrigan haunts. It staked out the Syracuse geriatrics center where his mother was resident. It searched convents in New York and Baltimore. It burst in on the wedding of two activist-friends in Baltimore; when a balloon accidentally popped, agents whipped out guns. There was no finding him. Berrigan, meanwhile, was peppering the upperworld with interviews, statements, and articles that broadened his philosophy of dissent and strengthened ties between segments of the radical left. Hardly a week went by without another Berrigan visitation on television or in the pages of one or another prominent publication: *Saturday Review, Village Voice, Commonweal, The New Yorker, Christian Century, New York Review of Books, New York Times Magazine.* On a warm summer Sunday he surfaced in Philadelphia, and in First United Methodist Church he preached for 20 minutes his message that "it is impossible to remain a Christian and abide by the law of the land." Then, he was out a side door, into an automobile, and back to the underground.

Five days later he was addressing by tape a rally in Wilmington, Delaware at which some 300 persons publicly accepted legal and moral responsibility for draft board raids in several Delaware cities. The tape, played also to a New York press conference, urged on hearers "the courage to wage peace," and stressed that such a commitment "requires the moral equivalent of the suffering required to wage war."

A network of some 200 persons abetted the homeless Berrigan along the Boston-Washington corridor, transporting him, bunking him, making the next contact— usually via pay telephone: "In the name of peace, will you harbor this man? Will you share his legal jeopardy?" There was no plea in this request, no apology for the asking. Like Berrigan himself, the people around him had no compunction about placing demands on conscience; in fact they might have been a lot blunter. Nor was Berrigan running scared in the underground. Quite the opposite, he seemed to relish the role of fugitive.

"We are summoned to act in unison with our friends," Dan Berrigan wrote at one point in the underground, "to join in conspiracy, in jeopardy, in illegal nonviolent actions, to hotten up the scene, wherever we are." The summons was edgy and, in the legal sense, perhaps incriminatory. But the essential Berrigan conviction remained that any activity which protected life, most especially innocent life, was and is life-serving.

Inevitably it all came to an end. In August, against the advice of those who had helped organize the underground, Berrigan went to Block Island, off Rhode Island, to the home of Dr. William Stringfellow, the lawyer and Episcopalian theologian, and the late Anthony Towne, the poet and satirist—old friends. He settled into a one-room study that was once a stable for horses. He may as well have plunked himself down in the middle of Time Square with all exits blocked. The FBI tracked him there. On August 11, Berrigan's fifth day on the island, a Coast Guard cutter suddenly blockaded the harbor. A dozen or so FBI agents, incongruously posing as bird watchers—it was a foul day—took up posts in the bushes about the house. Berrigan saw them; the chase was over. He came out, introduced himself, and said, "God bless."

Berrigan was whisked into custody. A news picture caught him being led off between two dour-faced agents. Widely reproduced, the photo prompted essayist Dwight Macdonald and Protestant theologian Robert McAfee Brown to similar observations: the handcuffed Berrigan, grinning, was the free man; the agents, the bound ones.

—8—

The prison experience was hard on Dan Berrigan. He was assigned as a dental assistant, doing a variety of jobs: taking and mounting X-rays, cleaning instruments, helping out at the dental chair, cleaning up afterward—in general, being available to two professional dentists. Religious superiors kept lines open. The provincial of the New England Jesuit province sent a touching letter of greetings to "a suffering and prophetic brother," and the general of the Jesuit order, Father Pedro Arrupe, came to visit. Having his brother Phil in the same prison was consolation and strength. The two organized Bible-study groups and conducted a loosely structured Great Books program. There were also "endless sessions" with individuals. Neither Berrigan brother functioned officially as a chaplain, but "to the extent that chaplaincies have viability and recognition among the prisoners," Dan says, "they were the chaplains at Danbury." "Those other birds were either despised or ignored," he comments.

Berrigan would not have had his role otherwise; in other words he would not have wanted, nor would he have accepted some kind of designation as chaplain. "The way the prisons are conducted, our best bet was to be in an adversary role," he explains. "That was our access to the prisoners. That was the way they could trust us—that we were in the same boat with them."

Yet on one occasion he would have welcomed the opportunity to function formally as a chaplain. An invitation came to baptize in prison the newborn child of a Vietnamese couple who were friends of a friend. Berrigan thought an enormously powerful moment was implied by the invitation, and he was anxious to perform it. This was not to be. The request got "chewed up" between the administration of the prison, Washington, the local religious bureaucracy (the area's bishop was involved), the parish downtown, the prison chaplain, and so on. The word back was a sharp no. There were no reasons offered, no explanations. Some time later, Berrigan, still troubled by the refusal, approached the prison chaplain to seek out his version of what happened. He tells of the incident in *Absurd Convictions, Modest Hopes,* a book of conversations that he did with the author Lee Lockwood:

"One morning after Mass I approached him on the subject. I was met by his blank stare, a classic one, which was his typical response to all prisoners, especially when any decision was required that would demand balls on his part. He said, as I recall, that the decision had been reached 'by chancery' that no baptism could occur in prison. When I inquired as to his own feelings on the decision, he suddenly, in a rare and unexpected flash, burst out in anger. It was a moment of truth, a moment of importance for both of us. First of all, it proved that he had some temper left, some reaction to me; then it showed, I think, his deep cowardice and contempt for the prisoners.

"He said to me, 'I concurred in this decision; I agreed with it completely.' And when I inquired as to why, 'Because prison is not a fit place for a child's baptism.' Then he yelled out again, as I recall, something like, 'Baptisms belong in church, and prisons are prisons.' So I wondered mildly aloud whether or not he thought Calvary would have been a fit place to have a Mass, and then walked away."

Berrigan developed no respect for the prison chaplains at Danbury. The same was true of Phil. "We went to Mass on Sunday with the men," Dan says of himself and his brother. "We received Communion with them. And we did that even though we'd have liked to wear ear plugs during the sermons. We *really* had to fight our hatred of the priests and ministers. I say *hatred* advisedly. We saw them wearing the spiritual uniform of bankrupt and corrupt power, playing that game, refusing to step aside from it even on the most atrocious occasions of human need. We'd go to one of them when a crisis occurred, and the chaplain would say, 'I can't do anything. I'll have to go to the warden.' And I'd say, 'Does Christ go to Caesar to vindicate human need? If he does we're in the wrong boat.'"

If the religious scene in the prison upset him so much, why did he and Phil go to the regularly scheduled religious services? "We went," says Berrigan, "in order to read the gospel with the men, to receive Communion, to be part of that humiliation."

If Danbury was hard on the soul, it was harder on the body. Berrigan entered prison suffering from a "herniated esophagus," an ulcer condition that required milk and a bland, greaseless diet. Prison food is not hospital food, so that condition was aggravated. Then he came down with an arthritic elbow that required periodic cortisone shots, and toward the end of his stay he developed pains in the lower back which were subsequently diagnosed as a form of arthritis of the spine.

That was not all. There was a dramatic illness, one that almost claimed Berrigan's life and which put prison officials in a panic from the warden on down; it is not good, it goes without saying, to have one's most celebrated inmate die on one's hands. The illness occurred while Berrigan was undergoing routine dental work on June 9, 1971. The assistant administering Novocain accidentally pierced an artery, setting off a "massive allergic shock" to the respiratory system. At first it was thought that Berrigan had suffered a heart attack. He went unconscious, his breathing momentarily stopped, and he was rushed by ambulance to Danbury Hospital, where he was kept in intensive care for several days. When the diagnosis was finally made it all seemed too ironic to Berrigan. He thought of Merton and the electric shock that killed him. "And then this absurd needle with me. It was strange—both of us in our 50th year! And both of us in exile." Berrigan may have been 50 at the time, but actually Merton was 53 when he died. However, 50 is close enough. Merton's death was terribly premature. That was Berrigan's point. Was his own also to be premature, when so much remained to be done?

Fate decided otherwise.

In August, 1971, Berrigan became eligible for parole and was granted a hearing. Parole was denied, no explanation given. In January, however, the U.S. Board of Parole in Washington, D.C. agreed to hear his case on the ground that there was "new evidence" bearing on Berrigan's health. To everyone's surprise, parole was granted. The board said it acted on health considerations. Berrigan said he was being released as it was "politically embarrassing" for authorities to keep him in prison any longer. He walked out February 24, 1972.

3
New Elements in
the Equation

—1—

In his 1970 book *No Bars to Manhood,* Daniel Berrigan observed that he was one who "enjoyed all the fruits that America offers those fortunate to make it within her system." He had indeed made it big. He had career, income, purpose. Intellectual recognition was his, including literary recognition. Marianne Moore said she read "with reverence *any*thing" that Berrigan wrote. Phyllis McGinley commented that he offered his readers no little nosegay of pleasant pieties. "But there is a garden here," she added, "sternly cultivated, rewarding in all its seasons." Thomas P. McDonnell, later a Berrigan baiter, observed that "no one but Péguy had dared with more success to put words into the mouth of God."

As his books appeared one upon another, the *Saturday Review* called Berrigan "a bracing tonic." The prestigious *New York Review of Books* advised that "one who wishes to know what an authentically Christian response to the questions of our time is like would be wise to listen to Father Berrigan." *Commonweal* enthused over his "memorable lyric simplicity."

Berrigan's very first book, a 1957 volume of poems entitled *Time Without Number,* was honored by the Academy of American Poets with its Lamont Poetry Award, and three 1970 books (*No Bars to Manhood, The Trial of the Catonsville Nine,* and *Trial Poems*) won the annual Melcher Book Award of the Unitarian Universalist Association. The citation for the Melcher award was written by Herbert A. Kenny, himself a poet who had once presented poetry readings with Berrigan; it cited Berrigan "because in both his personal life and in his writings [he] has made a sustained and eloquent affirmation on behalf of mankind in jeopardy, and a fearless and continuing protest against all the powers that make genocidal war and deprave man for profit and power." In 1971, the Thomas More Association in Chicago named Berrigan the winner of its Thomas More Medal for the most distinquished contribution to Catholic literature during that year.

It was a time when publishers would take almost anything that Berrigan chose to put together; the question of quality was largely in his own hands and his own sense of things. Readers by the thousands awaited his new books.

Elements of that happy state of affairs were to change, however, partly by choice and partly as a result of events that placed some tarnish on the shining armor. The choice part is easier to speak about. Berrigan switched from front-line commercial publishers to small houses, which, however good, operated on another level of prestige and among a much smaller audience. It was a change that began to evidence itself around 1970, when Berrigan turned to Beacon Press. He had been publishing with Doubleday, Macmillan, Coward-McCann, and Random House. But now he felt uncomfortable with large publishing houses, several of which had become part of the multicorporate world, which Berrigan regarded with suspicion for being, by his readings, exploitive of people and resources. He talked his qualms over with his brother Phil and with others, and came to the conclusion that he would be more at ease with smaller houses, publishers such as

Beacon, Abington, Seabury, Templegate. The decision markedly lessened Berrigan's visibility among the reading public and accounted for a drop in his book royalties, but at least, he says he had the satisfaction of knowing that he wasn't taking money that was "tainted or had been exploited elsewhere." The toughest thing about the decision, he remarks, is that it meant breaking off working relationships with editors who were and are still close friends.

As for the developments that were to alter the popular image, they involved the 1971 Harrisburg conspiracy trial, a 1973 speech before the Association of Arab-American University Graduates, and Berrigan's defense of values that ran counter to some radically new feminist trends, particularly with respect to abortion. Each of these developments was to cost Berrigan dearly—in the peace movement, in the Jewish community, and among women, constituencies that until now had been solidly his.

—2—

Ironically, the Harrisburg conspiracy trial did not involve Dan Berrigan directly, although as the trial shaped up it appeared that it would. On November 27, 1970, he was cited by FBI director J. Edgar Hoover as a "principal" leader in a plot to blow up underground electrical conduits and steam pipes serving government buildings in Washington, D.C. He was also linked by Hoover to the "concocting"—his word—of a scheme to kidnap an unnamed high White House official. The official, it developed, was Richard Nixon's presidential adviser, Henry A. Kissinger. As for the bombing, it was planned, said Hoover, "to disrupt federal government operations." Kissinger, on the other hand, was to be held as ransom in a demand on the United States to end bombing operations in Southeast Asia and to release all political prisoners.

The scheme was so bizarre, so exotic that people right and left suspected Hoover of doing some concocting of his own. Primarily he was suspected of acting out of animus for the activist left, an old bête noir of his. "The main objective is a simple but deadly one," said attorney William Kunstler, "to destroy the peace movement by creating caricatures of those who oppose the war in Southeast Asia." Hoover's motives were thought also to be part ploy—aimed at securing funding for some 1,000 additional FBI agents for his bureau. He had made his allegations, after all, before a Senate appropriations sub-committee, a curious body before which to lay out so seri-ous a plot, even if it was in closed session. Not a few thought Hoover had gone just plain nuts.

Incredible as the allegations seemed, formal charges were served up by the FBI. The "conspirators" were labeled as a group the East Coast Conspiracy to Save Lives. After several shifts in cast, seven persons actually came to trial on charges of "conspiracy to commit crimes against the United States." Dan Berrigan was not among the sev-en. His "leadership" role in the alleged plot had been gradually downgraded, from co-leader to co-conspirator to nonparticipant. Philip Berrigan and Elizabeth McAlis-ter, then still a religious of the Sacred Heart of Mary, were, however, among the seven, and this was to prove fateful for Dan. The other defendants were two Baltimore priests, Father Joseph Wenderoth and Father Neil McLaughlin; Anthony Scoblick, a former priest; his wife, Mary Cain, a former nun; and Eqbal Ahmad, a Pakastani

Moslem who had been a resident of the United States for a dozen years and who was active in opposition to the war in Vietnam.

The government's case did not go well. There were embarrassing disclosures of extralegal investigative dealings on the part of law-enforcement agencies—which came as no surprise; Dan Berrigan had himself been illegally bugged by the FBI as far back as 1966. Further there was ineptness in the way the case was prosecuted, and maybe even a touch of hysteria. At one point, the chief prosecutor labeled the priests and nuns whom he sought to convict as worse than underground chieftains who live off murder, vice, corruption, and drugs.

Whatever, between superseding indictments, dropped counts, lost cases, and reversals on appeal, the government won convictions against only two of the seven defendants—Philip Berrigan and McAlister—and then on the relatively minor legal charge of smuggling letters to one another through prison walls. The letters were conveyed between the two by a prison trusty with "study release" privileges at nearby Bucknell University. (Berrigan was then at Lewisburg Federal Prison.) What neither Berrigan nor McAlister realized was that the trusty was an informant, that their letters were being turned over to authorities, copied, and then moved on.

If the letters were minor in a legal sense, they were anything but minor in political and psychological senses. They exploded like a bombshell on the public, as they had earlier on the defendants themselves when they gained access to some of the materials upon which the government was basing its case. "None of us knew about the letters," Wenderoth would say, "none of us knew how many there were. Believe it or not, none of us really ever knew what the contents of these letters were until we saw them in xeroxed form from the U.S. government."

The letters made clear that Hoover's Senate subcommittee testimony was not spun from whole cloth. In a *Time* magazine cover story appearing on the eve of the trial, Dan was quoted as saying there was "absolutely nothing" to the allegations, and Phil was quoted earthily as saying "it was all bullshit." It turned out, however, that there indeed had been some kind of conspiring, and there had been talk of making a citizen's arrest of Henry Kissinger. The latter possibility came up at a meeting of a small group of the activists in Connecticut, and was quickly dropped both on practical and moral grounds. The letters, however, gave no hint of the sheer tentativeness of the talk and went on to present as an accomplished fact matters that were merely conversational. "This," McAlister said later, "I can only attribute to my sense of purpose—which was to reassure Phil." Whatever the reason, the effects were devastating.

Probably even more devastating, at least in terms of the Catholic left, was the disclosure that Phil Berrigan and McAlister had a secret relationship. It did not help matters that Phil had been an ardent defender of clerical celibacy. For instance, in May of 1969, only a month before his secret marriage to McAlister, he was declaring celibacy to be "crucial in the priesthood as an aid for revolutionary lifestyle"; celibacy, he continued, "can be a great freedom in a public forum." To many it all seemed so much hypocrisy.

Later, when the two announced their marriage, they conceded that the reasons for their secrecy, however strong, were perhaps mistaken. "At first, we wanted our relationship to clarify itself without pressure," they said in the 1973 statement making public their marriage. "In the midst of that process, Philip went to prison [April, 1970]. At that point, public disclosure was impossible, since it would have put the total burden of explanation upon Elizabeth. Later in the year, we did speak to friends and family, and their pain at our secrecy revealed that that had been an error in judgment on our part. As the Harrisburg trial approached, we contemplated disclosing our union but we felt that a free admission on our part would confuse both the substance of the trial and our relationship itself. Following the trial and up to the point of Philip's release in December [1972], the separation of prison further prevented any public acknowledgement. Since that time we have sought opportunities to publicize it and to share it with friends."

The explanation, when it came, did not mend matters with all. Damage had been done, and it touched the movement as a whole, fragmenting a sizable part of it. Cynics had a field day. This was the kind of disclosure they obviously longed for, and they made the most of it. Philip and Elizabeth were pilloried by the righteous. For friends and supporters, it was another story. There was "shock and pain," says Meconis. People were disillusioned, disconsolate, puzzled. A few felt betrayed, and far and wide not a few wondered: One "holy outlaw" had proved to be somewhat less holy than thought. Might not the others? Might not Dan Berrigan himself?

In point of fact, Dan Berrigan was as much in the dark about what was taking place as were Wenderoth and others at the inner core of the movement. Nevertheless, years later he remains marked by Harrisburg in the public consciousness. A young man, perhaps 30, was told of this book project. "Oh, I remember Dan Berrigan," he commented. "He's the guy who wanted to kidnap Kissinger."

The supreme irony is that Dan Berrigan, far from being an accomplice in the so-called Harrisburg conspiracy and conversant with all its far-reaching particulars, was actually a casualty of one aspect of them. For the letters that moved back and forth between his brother and McAlister put the FBI on his trail and resulted in his capture on Block Island. The vital clue was furnished by a McAlister letter.

Berrigan was asked by Lee Lockwood how he felt on learning this news. His response evidenced a characteristic concern for family feelings; it was full of understanding and of charity:

"Well, I think my feeling was a mild sense of relief. The question had long ceased to be an important one, except as a matter of closing off one period of my life. And of closing off a number of rather wounding speculations that had been going on among my friends.... Everyone was speculating with great fervor at the time, and the wildest rumors were circulating. Certain people within our circle were even accused of lapses of vigilance. So I was happy that the question was closed, that it was a matter of, let's say, a rather imprudent reference to myself and my friends, and nothing more."

—3—

On October 19, 1973, Dan Berrigan addressed the sixth annual convention of the Association of Arab-American University Graduates in Washington, D.C., and the consequences of the Harrisburg trial were for him as nothing compared to the consequences of that speech. This was the speech in which Berrigan stated that if he were a "conscientious Jew" living then in Israel, he would have to live much as he was living in the United States—that is, "in resistance against the state." Berrigan spoke out of his convictions, and what was described as "outraged love" of Israel. "I do not believe," he said early in his remarks, that "it is the destiny of human flesh to burn." The speech was a disaster for his standing among Jews and pro-Israeli people generally.

Berrigan thought he was not "taking sides" in his speech. "I am sick of 'sides,' he said, "which is to say, I am sick of war; of wars hot and cold; and all their approximations and metaphors and deceits and ideological ruses. I am sick of the betrayal of the mind and the failure of compassion and the neglect of the poor. I am sick of foreign ministers and all their works and pomps. I am sick of torture and secret police and the apparatus of fascists and the rhetoric of leftists. Like Lazarus staggering from his grave . . . I can only groan, 'We have had enough of all that, we have been through all that.' "

Thus, declared Berrigan, he would offer "no apologia for the Arab states any more than I do for Israel." Accordingly, while he welcomed news of an Egyptian cease-fire proposal, he did so while opposing many aspects of the Egyptian regime, and of the sheikdoms, and of Jordan and Syria. "We must take into account their capacity for deception," he commented, "which is remarkable even in our world. We must take into account their contempt for their own poor, a contempt that would be called legendary if it were not horrifyingly modern. We must take into account their willingness to oil the war machinery of the superpowers, making them accomplices of American war criminals. We must take into account their crudity, masked only by their monumental indifference to the facts of the world."

This was potent criticism, and, according to people who were there, the atmosphere was electric. To be critical of the Arabs before an audience of Arabs in a situation of war was, as one person expressed it, courageous almost to the point of foolhardiness. But this Arab criticism went largely unnoticed by the media and the public. It was blinded out by reaction to Berrigan's criticism of the state of Israel, what he called its "settler ethos," the reliance on "domestic repression, cruelty, [and] militarism," and the state's responsibility for having created "one and a half million refugees." It was blinded further by Berrigan's charging American Jewish leaders with "ignoring the Asian holocaust in favor of [obtaining] economic and military aid to Israel." As Jim Forest was to write in *Fellowship*, "the remarks on Israel . . . were a dirge of mourning for that state's having become so similar to the morally-hollow, state-worshiping 'Christendom' with which Berrigan had been jousting for years: that Bible-boasting public 'order' whereby the survival of the state becomes life's first and most obvious priority, thus making necessary a final reliance on war, with all its ideological underpinnings."

The Jewish and liberal pro-Israeli communities were not pleased. Sales of his books plummeted. Berrigan was denounced, heckled when he appeared before audiences. He was charged with the "new antisemitism"—regarded as Christian indifference or insensitivity toward Isreal, bound up in a Christian incapacity or unwillingness to comprehend the necessity of the existence of Israel to Jewish safety and survival throughout the world. People wondered, as Michael Novak did in *Commonweal*, whether the record of American priests who become active in politics would "once again end in fanaticism, under the guise of 'prophecy.'"

In the midst of this controversy, Berrigan was scheduled to receive the Gandhi Peace Prize. The prize was to be presented by Rev. Donald S. Harrington, prominent Unitarian churchman and chairman of the Liberal Party of the State of New York. He announced he would not do it. Then a poll was initiated among directors of the peace prize, seeking re-evaluation of their choice. Berrigan refused the award, objecting to the poll.

As for the talk, even close friends were hard put to defend it through and through, or the circumstances in which it was delivered. "The talk was flawed," said Forest, one of the closest of the close. "While its widest audience has been its readers, one regrets that a talk so heavy with criticisms of Israel was heard first by a group so well-disposed to such criticsm." Forest found the imagery and analogies "too absolute, too damning." The portrayal of Jewish leadership's capitulation to Washington and the administration of Richard Nixon was, he added, "too sweeping." Finally, said Forest, "the equation of Jew with outsider and resister," whereby Berrigan saw himself as a Jew of sorts, "is revelatory of his own vocation within the Christian tradition, but hardly establishes a foothold for communication with Jews."

It became apparent that Berrigan realized some of this himself, after the fact. In a televised conversation with Hans Morganthau, he was asked, "If you had to make that speech again, would you make it the way you have made it? Or have you learned something from the experience?" Berrigan responded: "Well, I've learned a great deal, not merely about myself, but about the community, and specifically the American Jewish community, and that has made me ... very sober about the whole question .... I would think of nothing essential that I would want to retract. I would want to add something which I think we've gotten into very briefly. I don't think I conveyed my sense of love for Israel and for the Jewish people, which is very deep in me. I said at one point that this was an act of love, but it was outraged love. But I should have developed that more. And as you brought up earlier, I think I should have spoken more about my admiration for the social achievements and the agricultural and industrial achievements of Israel, especially in those early years when it was so difficult . . . ."

Subsequently, Berrigan went to the Middle East and spent several weeks talking with Israelis and Arabs, and visiting the Palestinian camps. The results did not persuade him that he was wrong on his basic premises. He still insists that there is a critical distinction between the people of the covenant, indeed between the whole prophetic and historic content of the Old Testament on the one hand, and the state of Israel on the other. Unless one keeps such a distinction, and states it firmly and publicly when required, one is only creating another sacred hegemony, technologized, armed to the teeth, automatically exempt from the criticism that should fall on any state—this he would maintain now, as he once did to *Time* in an interview which the magazine chose not to publish. Not surprisingly, when two West Bank Palestinian mayors were expelled by the Israeli government from their homes May 3, 1980 Berrigan joined in a public condemnation of the action as "a violation of basic democratic and internationally-recognized human rights."

Berrigan is insulted by any suggestion that his position with respect to Israel is antisemitic, latent or overt, new strand or old. He would be as critical of his own church, his own people, if the situation were reversed. Indeed, precisely as a Catholic he may feel that he has an instinctual understanding of the Zionist mind. "Catholics," he argued in the aborted *Time* interview, "wouldn't notably differ from Zionists if, for example, we still had a hold on the old papal states. There would be the same feeling, a kind of quasi-religious feeling about a certain turf. Catholics would say, 'Let's send in troops, save the pope's acreage.'" Berrigan would denounce that too. But would that, he asks by implication, make him anti-Catholic?

It distresses Berrigan that people he loves, admires, respects have harbored negative impressions stemming back to the 1973 talk to the Arab-American association. The hurt is deep; it is a spiritual as well as emotional hurt. But he stands by his principles. Moral continuity is important, he would say, whatever the personal consequences. And the consequences for him have been very real.

Berrigan's media eclipse can be traced directly to the speech before the Association of Arab-American University Graduates. Hitherto he had had rather immediate access to any media form, whether the press, television, radio talk shows, or mainline book review outlets, such as *The New York Review of Books* and the *New York Times*. In Berrigan's words, "There just fell a blanket over all that stuff." Among other things affected were sales of his books; thousands of people stopped buying Daniel Berrigan.

Berrigan is cautious in attributing reasons for the media blackout of him, and he rejects the notion of conspiracy. He does say: "There is a heavy pro-Israel and media control here in New York. I guess that's no news to anybody. It's only very, very recently that we have begun to learn on any large scale that the Palestinian people exist. So that I committed for those days a really unpardonable sin in the eyes of the New York media. This didn't penetrate elsewhere, when I went elsewhere. The power of the media isn't as great elsewhere."

But it penetrated in New York, and New York being the media capital of the United States, it was as if the main gates of media interest were shut against him. They have opened a little since, but not a whole lot. On September 9, 1980, he and Philip and six other peace activists entered a classified area of the General Electric Space Division in King of Prussia, Pennsylvania. They went in as people answering the summons of the prophets Isaiah and Micah to beat swords into ploughshares, and with hammers they put dents in the nose cones of two Minuteman 3 intercontinental ballistic missiles. (General Electric makes more than food blenders.) They also splashed human blood and scattered ashes over tools and documents. Television cameras recorded their arrest, and there was re-entry into national evening news broadcasts. But the *New York Times,* the supreme arbiter of news that's fit to print, gave the incident a scant two paragraphs in its "Around the Nation" round-up. In Chicago, the incident was worth a three-column headline over story and picture.

—4—

Less anguishing personally, but disconcerting nonetheless, is that many women, Catholic feminists among these, have discounted Berrigan in recent years. Of course, part of Berrigan's problem is his own maleness. Women have been put upon for so long by the male element of the species that many of them understandably look upon males as oppressors, just for reason of their maleness; at the same time they look exclusively to their own gender for inspiration, leadership, and direction. Among such women, Berrigan would not command a large audience, however much he may abhor and fight against sexism in society and in the church, and however profeminist his positions may be on certain controversial issues, as the ordination of women as priests. In point of fact, he strongly favors the idea of women priests, thinks that Pope John Paul II is less than helpful in talking the way he does about women, and would support any Catholic bishop who dared to proceed against authority and ordain women. It irks him, for example, that the fate of Father Robert Drinan, S.J., the congressman deposed by the Pope, should have been a more disturbing matter for most within his order than that of Father William Callahan, S.J., a priest who was disciplined for his championing of the ordination of women. The Drinan question Berrigan considers "totally superficial in any long-range understanding of things"; the Callahan question he considers central both on the human and institutional level. As a priest Berrigan is willing to share the altar with women—and has, as at a recent ecumenical meeting in Kentucky. He is also willing to be a member of a congregation which has women alone at the altar. For all of this, however, there is no acceptance for Berrigan into the good graces of the militant feminists.

There are some small problems, probably including language. Berrigan is respectful toward the classical language of the Bible—that God is "he," or God is the "father." Similarly, though he uses everyday language with great sensitivity and strives to avoid the sexism which exists in it, he declines to bend to points where he feels speech or the written word become "atrocious" in sound or syntax.

But all that is minor. What has hurt Berrigan most

among radicalized women of the left is his position on abortion. He's against it, and has been consistently. He strives conscientiously to bring "a certain humanity, a certain amount of understanding" to his position; in other words, he is not combative and accusatory in the fashion of many pro-life Catholics. But he is opposed nonetheless.

"I think abortion is as serious an ethical question as capital punishment or as murder," he says, "and with all the respect and the sympathy toward women that I can muster I believe it is wrong tactically that people isolate this question among women, just as it is not helpful to isolate the war question among men. We're all in this leaking boat together. Every conception involves a man, and every war involves women, and let's act as though it's true." In his opinion, to say that abortion is a woman's issue—the "our bodies, ourselves" sort of argument—is parallel to saying that war is a man's problem, or that capital punishment is a legal problem, or that the poor are an economic problem. "This is putting rats in a labyrinth," he comments. "What we have to work toward is the realization that every human being belongs to a community. This approach cuts across the stereotypes."

Likewise, he rejects the feminist notion that abortion is "liberating." He says he has never met a person involved in an abortion who is not haunted by that memory.

Berrigan is adamant on the subject. He is convinced women are doing a great disservice by isolating the fate of the unborn as their own problem. "This is biologically and spiritually absurd," he counters. "Ironically, such an idea also plays into the hands of the machos. It isolates the woman at just that point where male responsibility needs to be jolted."

Berrigan spoke in great detail of his feelings about abortion in a 1979 issue of *Reflections,* a newsletter for women and men who have experienced abortion. "I come to the abortion question by way of a long, long experience with the military and the mainline violence of the culture, expressed in war," he said. "There I see the dead end of disrespect and contempt for life; the main project—in fact, the only project—is murder. So I go from the Pentagon and being arrested there, to the cancer hospital, and then I think of abortion clinics, and I see an 'interlocking directorate' of death that binds the whole culture. That is, an unspoken agreement that we will solve our problems by killing people in certain ways; a declaration that certain people are expendable, outside the pale."

He confessed to his interviewer, Lucien Miller, that he found his campaign of resistance to war and to abortion emotionally draining: "It is a hell of a way to spend one's life, as I do, objecting to the killing of people. It is like being in the stone age, prehuman. You would like to be building human community with certain common presuppositions, and you can't. You can't. It is like living in a cave, sitting around the fire arguing whether we should go out and club people and eat them. As if this were a serious choice. When I meet those well-tailored, secure, professional people, especially religious people, indifferent to the hideous course of the world, I feel as though I don't belong in this world. I wonder where I do belong."

In this context he thinks back admiringly to the sisters at St. Rose's Free Home for Incurable Cancer. "I gain so much from the sisters," he exclaims. "Some have been there 50 years—walking a thin line among the dying, between hardening of heart, or collapsing amid the pain. You try to walk that line, because neither alternative would be helpful. To me that's life. You walk a thin line. Maybe that is what we are called to do today. I hope so, for that is what I do."

It is because many people are willing to walk the thin line that Berrigan has hope. "The hope," he says, "is parallel in all these issues—war, capital punishment, abortion—because the questions are literally matters of life and death. The hope is the minority that stands somewhere and lays out something for the unborn and born, and whose appeal is to a God of life. I am not appalled or terrified by America. My closest and dearest friends are anti-nuke and anti-abortion. I find that very healing. It keeps us going. Whether or not we can win in any of these areas, or turn the picture around is secondary. In the nature of things it is secondary. We are not called upon to play God, but just to be human. And to be human is to continue to struggle. And it is precisely out of the struggle that one grows in hope."

And what is the epitome of hope? It is in couples having children.

Berrigan was asked in a *U.S. Catholic* interview if he were a young person and just getting married, would he bring a child into a world about whose future he has such foreboding? His answer was an unqualified yes. "This is a most important sign of hope," he explained. "Maybe it's an illustration of the old text from Romans about what true hope is. We have to decide if we want to embody the fact that we believe we have a future. And a child is the most beautiful way of doing that that I know of."

4

Into A Seventh Decade

—1—

So the media have peeled away. The crowds do not follow adoringly as they once did. Daniel Berrigan can eat in restaurants without all eyes sneaking in his direction. He can travel in peace. It is a dividend of lower visibility. At destiny's end there are friends, admirers, kindred ideologues, but in transit there are the unseeing, unrecognizing eyes. It must be a relief, in a way—to have one's privacy back again. Berrigan uses every minute of it to advantage. He goes to movies—he calls himself a movie freak—often at a theater on 94th Street, just off Broadway, which features double-billings of the classics; Merton used to go there when he was at Columbia. He likes to cook for his friends, and he prides himself on some fish plates, vegetarian dishes, and desserts. He likes to get away to the country, and Block Island is a favorite piece of country, despite the memories of his capture there. He enjoys reunioning with family, relaxing with kin. But mostly he is a bear for work. He lectures, gives retreats, works at the cancer hospital, conducts college and university courses. And he writes—writes almost constantly. He writes in his apartment; he writes when he travels. "I like to write in airplanes," he says, "and I do it to stay sane in airports, to which I am frequently condemned and where I feel as though I were totally out of this world." In the shadow years of his 50s, he has been as active as a youth.

Berrigan's life is in a pattern with that of members of the

West Side Jesuit Community generally. "We find our own jobs. We try to be supportive of one another, and worship periodically and eat together; we have five meals a week in common in a common apartment which we rent. We are trying to find a new way of being in the order, I guess. We want to be less institutional and less under some kind of canopy of total support and total control," Berrigan explains. "It's rocky. It's difficult to keep the community together in New York. It's difficult keeping a sensible connection with the whole order, with the whole province, because a lot of people resent this and don't want Jesuits living this way." But he is making it. "It's much easier to be a Jesuit these days," he comments, "at least in this community." One reason perhaps is that there is more of a sense of value in what Berrigan is trying to say and do—at least to him it appears so.

Berrigan pays his own way in the order. He contributes to the common kitchen; buys his own wardrobe, pays his own rent—$325 a month. There's a good bit left over. "I make a lot of money," Berrigan confesses, adding that in round figures his annual income comes "probably closer to $30,000 a year" than $20,000. Most of the money comes from preaching, lecturing, giving retreats, and reading poetry around the country. "I soak the universities," he remarks unblushingly. "If they have the money, I really ask for it." That means a minimum of $500 for a campus appearance, and up to $1,000; plus expenses. The money is not turned over to a Jesuit treasury. "I worked out an arrangement with the order after I was in jail," Berrigan declares. "I said to them I didn't want my income going to the institution. I wanted to be able to help people in the peace movement, prisoners, and other folks. I said I would like to be an element in the conscience of the province and

give money away." And that is what he does. He helps
Jonah House. He performed a wedding of a lifer at Attica
Prison around 1978, and he has been helping the man's
family ever since. "He married a divorced woman with
three children," Berrigan remarks. "We have hopes of his
getting out one day, but in the meantime the wife and
children are in great poverty." Then there is the peace
movement; there is always need of money there. "I have a
wide continental friendship in the peace movement," he
continues. "People have just been sentenced again on the
West Coast to a year in jail—Jim Douglass and other
people." Their families have to be helped out.

Specific example of Berrigan's generosity: There is a Dr.
Arthur J. Kraus, a professor of Polish-Jewish background,
who was fired from the faculty of City College of New
York back in 1933 after conducting a protest march and
going on a hunger strike to protest fascism in Europe and
isolationism in the United States. For 35 years he fought
for vindication and rehabilitation, and finally in 1970
the city Board of Education issued him an apology,
the state legislature voted a Dr. Kraus bill, and then-
Governor Nelson E. Rockefeller signed a bill amending
the administrative code of the city of New York so that a
pension could be provided Kraus as a person "discharged
without just cause." The signing of the bill took place at an
elaborate ceremony in gubernatorial offices in mid-
Manhattan. I was involved in the Kraus case, and at one
particularly desperate point in Kraus' hard life—his pension was not enough to support him; in fact, it only lessened his welfare check—I put him in touch with Dan Berrigan. I thought Berrigan would be able to supply some
sort of ideological comfort. He did, and material assistance
as well.

Berrigan's instant interest in the Kraus case is clue to the broad scope of his concern about injustices. He may theorize that one cannot do everything, but he certainly does seek to do something, seemingly wherever in the world the injustices may exist. At what turned out to be great personal injury, he became involved in the Palestinian cause; he has persisted in the cause, despite the heavy personal consequences. Similarly, in late summer of 1980, he was in Ireland along with his brothers Phil and Jerry, demonstrating and fasting on behalf of members of the Provisional Irish Republican Army being held on H Block at Long Kesh in Northern Ireland, as well as on behalf of their female counterparts imprisoned in an Armagh jail. That too may cost him some more support.

One does not have to be a partisan of the Provisional IRA or a believer in the use of violence, a penchant of the "Provos," to understand Berrigan's interest in the prisoners. To be concerned for the imprisoned is a Christian act, a corporal work of mercy actually. Regardless of what the prisoner has been charged with or convicted of, the prisoner remains a human being, a person entitled to decent treatment, if nothing more. Berrigan is anxious to see that the prisoner receives this. "There's nothing in the world easier than to take prisoners," he says, "and nothing easier once you take them than maltreating them, torturing them, working out your hatred and frustrations on them."

As a prisoner once for a stretch of more than two years and for shorter periods on any number of occasions—he has not kept an exact tally of his arrests and incarcerations—Berrigan is persuaded he knows whereof he speaks. Thus he is willing to go long distances, to cross oceans on behalf of prisoners, and to Ireland especially.

"Obviously one can't go everywhere in the world on behalf of prisoners," he states. "One would have to go to 60 or 70 nations at least. But for reasons of my own background and reasons of the church, the Irish thing is very close." There is also an element of gratitude in his Irish witness. Right after he and Phil were released from Danbury prison an Irish linen handkerchief arrived from the prisoners at Long Kesh, hand-decorated and containing a moving dedication to the brothers. "I never forgot that the Long Kesh prisoners knew about us, and did that thing for us as prisoners," he remarks.

Berrigan's fasting in Ireland, his taking up of the Palestinian refugee cause, his opposition to the arms race—activities such as these fuel the contention that the end of the war in Vietnam left Berrigan politically and ideologically stranded. The contention continues that Berrigan's witness has therefore become scatter-shot, and that in an attempt to maintain a continuum of involvement, he is alighting desperately on issues that bear little or no relationship to one another and that are nowhere near so cosmically important as he would have them. One hears this criticism even from old partisans, people who are grateful to him and respect him yet for the witness made against the war in Vietnam. It is unfair criticism, however, and it is criticism that ignores some vital personal history. Berrigan is "not still fighting the war," as one critic put it to me. A stronger case can be made that Berrigan's antiwar activities grow out of a philosophy that took shape years ago; that the war only accented the strength of his philosophical convictions; and that his present concerns are remarkably consistent with his philosophical past.

As an example, Berrigan fights against the arms race: "Scientific effort spirals upward, narrowing toward a cone;

at the vent stands one man's control or one nation's pride. In such a process, the good of the person and the good of the community are inevitably obscured as values and goals. In the process of the cold war, moreover, each stage in the process is looked on as a value in itself, a kind of teasing invitation. We have gotten so far, why not further? Since a breakthrough has happened, why not a further one? Beyond any reasonable doubt, a further one is desirable. Let's make it."

This could be Berrigan just back from a 1980 demonstration at the Pentagon and satirizing the mind of the military scientists. In point of fact, it was Berrigan writing in *Fellowship* magazine in May, 1965—two-and-a-half years before his first arrest at the Pentagon; three years before the action at Catonsville; 15 years before his present involvements.

Berrigan can even point to a philosophical consistence between his opposition to the arms race and his concern for prisoners. "There's a connection that is hard to get people to draw," he admits. "Obviously the arms race is international by now. And the arms race inevitably is creating dictatorships and fascist governments, so you have more and more rounding up of political dissidents everywhere, and worse and worse treatment of prisoners, whether in South Korea or Chile or Argentina or Southern Africa. I mean, I've been on the prison question internationally for many years now—more years than I can count. I've always thought those things—international violence and international fascism—are always connected. Given the one, you have the other."

So Berrigan continues on, a kind of "easy rider," playing things loose in the sense of not getting stuck in age or institutions. The critics can say what they may. He knows what he thinks is right, and he plans to be about that business.

In this context, I asked Jerry Berrigan in Syracuse what the future held for the Berrigan brothers. He was quick in his answer: more resistance, more civil disobedience, more arrests, more time spent in jail. Dan says somewhat the same thing. "I couldn't think of anything more boring," he remarked to the question, "than to grow old at 98th Street or anywhere else . . . . I would define 'boring' as getting satisfied with being some kind of Jesuit professional in the old track . . . . But keeping life from getting boring are the awful things that are going on in the world, and being determined to do whatever one can at least to mitigate things for a few. That means more arrests and more jailing, and keeping at it. That's about all I can say."

One thing is for sure. The future will bring more contentions with his country, for Berrigan remains deeply embittered on many of our national conceptualizations. "So much of what we call daily life, human life, is concerned with death in a fashion that's very peculiar," he has commented. "For instance, we have all kinds of 'wars' declared against this or that aspect of death. We have a war on poverty, a war on cancer, a war on heart disease. There's even a war on war. These aspects of death around us, within us, are always conceived of as the great enemy which must be overcome so that we can get beyond disease, war, poverty—into what they like to think of as the good life, the real life, the life which has no death within it. And this dream continues. But it's always a kind of troubled and violent dream because it implies (and sometimes says openly) that, in order to make that leap, we have to make war on something or somebody. To attain anything like the truth of life, or a life with others, something is always in our way; and must be done away with, must be over-come.

"Of course the fact is that the culture is almost totally bankrupt of a vision of what a good life might be. We're ridden by consumerism, fear, violence, racism—all these terrible mythologies which forever put off any real vision. I find it interesting in the light of the scripture that, while the dream of the good life is forever delayed, death is always magnified: omnipresent, omnivorous, the shadowy other, the enemy. So we never really pay tribute to life at all, and never arrive at life. What we're really doing all the time is paying tribute to death. The eventuality of life is put off and put off and put off, because the obstacles and enemies multiply like piranhas, forever."

Berrigan's reading of America virtually guarantees his career as a resister. "Until the end of history we'll be waging a shadow war," he predicts. "The shadows are created by our own psyche in the image of death. In this itch for beatitude, which has nothing to do with God or our neighbor—in order to get nearer to that, we must kill all the time. In the pursuit of life, we are always dealing out death. War becomes the continual occupation and preoccupation in the minds of people who are purportedly trying to get to a better life.

"Speaking in biblical terms, God is superseded by the ape of God, which is actually personified death. This is the shrine at which we worship. This, I think, is the practical consequence of our war on life. Our real shrines are nuclear installations and the Pentagon and the war research laboratories. This is where we worship, allowing ourselves to hear the obscene command that we kill and be killed—a command which, it seems to me, is anti-Christ, is anti-God."

In the future he sees for himself as a priest-activist, very likely his will continue to be a lonesome voice. "There's a diabolic ecumenism at work," Berrigan maintains. "The mainline churches have joined this effort to make killing acceptable and normal—at least by silence." He doesn't exclude his own church.

—2—

For all his pessimism about America and the future, Dan Berrigan, in the new parlance, is very much a "laid back" person. He is of course a man of limited patience, a man who believes that each individual worth the salt must perform his or her saving act, in whatever way. Unlike some others on his scene, however, he is not a battering ram, one to high-pressure another into acting. The individual must make his or her own decision. Berrigan is cool and unflurried, and in person disarmingly calm, certainly in contrast to his writings, which can be angry, impatient, sometimes pure acid. In the printed word, it sometimes seems Berrigan is only a syllogism away from absolute incivility or, for that matter, from extreme physical, as distinct from measured, moral rebellion. Yet his touchstone remains the scriptures, and just when it seems that he might be going the "full route" as revolutionary, he reverts to biblical and Gandhian contexts.

Of late there appears to be a quality of Buddhist patience and resignation about the man, as if he sensed that the future belonged to his kind, if only by sorry vindication. Living among the Vietnamese Buddhist community-in-exile in Paris for several months in the mid-1970s helped cultivate these qualities. "In my prior religious experience, which was totally American and Christian, I simply had never in my life come upon such a large community so unified in the convictions of nonviolence, and people who were able to work that out beautifully, up close," he comments. He is convinced that much of the Vietnamese Buddhists' spiritual unity derived from the fact that they are a community of the poor. "They were so unwesternized," says Berrigan. "They didn't know what church and vestments might be. They simply had no access or interest in that." The experience of living in this community rubbed off strongly. "The further I get from that in time," he says, "the more important it becomes, and the more it falls into perspective that a substantial kind of rock dropped in my pond. The ripples just don't die. I guess what it comes down to is something like this: The Buddhists remain for me the exemplar of religious community that has not yielded before technique and violence. To me that is precious and even unique in this world."

Still, for all the admiration of Gandhi, the Buddhists and Eastern religious traditions, Berrigan remains very much the Christian Catholic, with roots in the Old Testament as well as the New, the latter not devoid of some conservative shoots. He is a Catholic, for instance, who can—and in a *U.S. Catholic* article did—defend the rosary: "The rosary takes us along the way [of Jesus and the saints] which the Book of Acts uses as another word for Christianity itself. A series of mysteries. Moments in the life of that moving target, Jesus. The short steps of the long-distant runner, where we too may savor (share?) his loneliness."

We need that, says Berrigan. He needs it: "I need to know that Jesus lived and died, and the manner of his living and dying. Call it medicinal; call it antidote. I need an antidote to America. I need to live and die in a manner different from the way I am commanded to live and die in a tin-can culture, a culture which manages by a marvelous sleight of hand to be at the same time lethal, ridiculous, and immensely seductive." The rosary helps in this regard. "The fifteen mysteries are a drama of the present, big as life, unfinished as today, untidy even."

The Berrigan roots reach out in the main, however, to the Jesus of the New Word, the Jesus who blessed the peacemakers in the Sermon on the Mount, who consoled the poor in spirit, and who angrily hurled the moneychangers out of the temple. As such, he is a person willing to take liberties with ecclesiastical laws. For instance, he has performed marriages of people who in the eyes of the church had no right to marry.

"It is a very serious thing to witness a marriage that the law of the church says should not be performed," he concedes. Although he is averse to becoming known as a "marrying cleric," he does so—or has done so—because, he says, he has "a sense of the overriding compassion of Christ with all sorts of people, including people who have had unfortunate and tragic marriages."

"I happen to think," he adds, "that marriage is the most debased and most misused and misunderstood of all the sacraments. That cuts a lot of ways, but it also cuts across the church's bad treatment of people." Accordingly he will independently decide to confer the blessing of the church in cases of special urgency. But, again, rarely. "I have work to do," he comments. The last time he witnessed an "illegal" marriage he says he "can't even remember."

Finally, some of Berrigan's roots reach out to the prophets of the Old Testament, and to not a few people he is something of the prophet incarnate, his voice crying out against the arms race, against the persistent drift to war, his voice incensed over the assault which all this represents on the human spirit and especially on the poor. In his book *The Prophets*, Rabbi Abraham Joshua Heschel defined a prophet as a man who feels fiercely: "God has thrust a burden upon his soul, and he is bowed and stunned before man's fierce greed . . . . The prophet is intent on intensifying responsibility, is impatient with excuse, contemptuous of pretense and self-pity. His tone, rarely sweet or caressing . . . his words . . . often slashing, even horrid, designed to shock rather than edify." Prophet or not, this is Daniel Berrigan the witness.

Berrigan is aware of the prophet talk, and he obviously stands in awe of the prophets of ancient Israel. He is not, however, so bumptious as to claim the prophet's mantle for himself. He would say he is merely trying to bring some sanity to the world, some sense of responsibility on the part of privileged society for the poor and the put-upon, some concern for the history of humankind. The prophet's concern is with history, Heschel has said. Stripped of trends and trappings, history is ultimately honest and bare, unadorned and devoid of poise. With respect to the last, so is Berrigan.

Berrigan thinks that those in high places of government are blind to the connection between world despair and world poverty on the one hand and the arms race on the other. He believes the country is headed toward war. But he is not without hope. "I think that God has intervened already in many ways to salvage nuclear catastrophe," he says. "We were very close to launching nuclear weapons during the Vietnam war."

His belief in divine intervention is quite literal. "Every day is a miracle," he continues. "We've been living in the hands of madmen for a long time, who have been willing to push buttons on the world. That includes the Kennedys. I don't really know why it hasn't happened. Sidney Lens in that book *The Day Before Doomsday* documents about 35 occasions since Hiroshima when we were close to using nuclear bombs. It hasn't occurred, and I can't put that down as any kind of conscience on the part of the leadership."

—3—

If anyone is the embodiment of the group that Father Andrew Greeley classifies as "Catholic radicals" and that Meconis in his book terms the "American Catholic left," it is Daniel Berrigan. There is not much argument about that. The argument is whether Berrigan makes a difference anymore, or indeed whether he ever did make a difference.

Taking the latter point first, he most certainly did make a difference on the issue that for years was central to his life and his priesthood: the war in Vietnam. Admittedly, not everyone would agree. Greeley argued the negative side of the case in the *New York Times* for February 19, 1971:

"The truth is that the Catholic 'radicals' don't make any difference at all. They have no popular support, they can deliver no bloc votes, they are totally incapable of effecting any social change, they have no impact on larger society— save for consuming considerable amounts of media space.

"On the contrary, all the available data suggest that Berrigan-style protests are counterproductive for the causes they support."

I would not be one to subscribe to that. To believe that

theory is to believe that the student demonstrators of the Vietnam period did not make a difference either. But, of course, they did.

I much prefer Meconis' conclusion: "In the final analysis the Catholic left may have failed to meet the dramatic goals expressed in its own rhetoric, but it did play an important part in eventually ending the war, ending the draft, and exposing abuses by the FBI. In addition, the movement had an important influence on the American Catholic church and conducted a valuable experiment in nonviolent direct action."

Berrigan is understandably reluctant to claim too much for himself or for the movement. But he does feel that the Catholic left movement counted.

"I think it was part of something, yeah," he comments. "Again, I'm trying to understand it from the point of view of a lot of other people. I wouldn't have any big opinion myself. But I think it was important for many, both here and in Vietnam—as we found out when we went there. Daniel Ellsberg talks about the reaction in government circles, and it is clear they were scared witless about it. They were outraged by it, and they had to take it into account. So I have always looked upon it as one modest activity that we joined with a lot of other good stuff, and the cumulative effect was quite powerful. I really think it can be shown that as far back as '68, Johnson was ready for nuclear war in Southeast Asia. It was common knowledge when [Zinn and I] went over there that there were tactical nuclear weapons in Vietnam and that the technicians had arrived. Certainly the Vietnamese were aware of that. Now the nuclear bombs weren't dropped; the tactical weapons weren't used. Something happened. I think they found it politically impossible to do what they otherwise wanted to do, and would have done."

This is one element of the equation.

Of greater concern to Berrigan is whether the movement and he himself had some impact on the church. "That is really my love and my desire," he explains, "to help Catholics especially to take a new look at something that I think was atrocious in our background. That is to say, in the 20th century, after Hiroshima, that there could be a just war, or that you could justify war."

So far as Catholics are concerned, Berrigan is persuaded that a corner has been turned. "Everywhere I go, I meet people—Catholics of every sort of range and description—who say things like this: that I stay in the church because of people like you; or I came back because of people like you; or I'm thinking about these things because of people like you. That keeps coming up all the time. I don't want to make too much of it, but what would have happened to people if we hadn't done what we did? Where would the church be? I don't think much would have changed. The people that we find seriously confronting things like civil disobedience on the nuclear question are invariably religious people. Now how do you evaluate that? I mean including civil disobedience; I don't mean apart from that—that's a big cultural mix. I mean people coming up through a Gandhian or Martin Luther King or Cesar Chavez or Dorothy Day tradition to say 'you've got to keep at this stuff today!' They are doing it because they are reading the Bible and praying, and have access to the sacraments and all that. Now that is really quite remarkable on any significant scale. And I hope we have a part in that."

In a sense the latter comment answers the question, "Does Dan Berrigan make a difference any more?" He does. To some his activities may seem foolhardy, mere gestures on a scene where gestures do not count for much. What is it to pour blood around the Pentagon or a General Electric missile plant? What is it to scatter ashes around? What is it to put some dents in some military hardware? The blood can be washed away, the ashes swept up, the hardware repaired or replaced. It's a big scene out there, as big as the world and financed as solidly as the United State Treasury. Nudges don't move mountains. Behemoths are not prodded by pin pricks.

But people do notice, and people eventually make the difference. It happened during the Vietnam years, and it could happen again. Maybe Daniel Berrigan, his brothers, those who support them and act with them will not be the direct instruments of a sweeping change in consciousness, in conscience, in military policy. But if the world is saved from itself—or, as Daniel Berrigan might word it, if it is saved from the United States and its armaments mania— then it is quite likely that Dan Berrigan will have been a factor.

The late Malcom X said somewhere that because he dared to go to the extremes he did, Martin Luther King was able to go as far as he did. Daniel Berrigan dares the extremes. History holds the answer to the ultimate effectiveness of this. History and himself, of course. The world is not going to disarm; the political prisoners are not all going to wake up tomorrow to a better day; nuclear power is not going to go away. But because of people like Dan Berrigan, nations may come to limit arms and bring whatever arms are necessary under a serious control; prisoners may receive somewhat better treatment—some prisoners, somewhere; there may even be an arrival at sanity with respect to peaceful uses of nuclear power. The only hope for any of these objectives is people willing to challenge the maximalists, those who would do anything because anything is possible. Daniel Berrigan is a challenger of maximalists.

—4—

The new decade was only nine months into its first year, the normal gestation period for new life, when the Berrigan prediction of a future of more resistance, more civil disobedience, more arrests, more time spent in jail had materialized. Dan and Phil were both in prison for the September 9 action at King of Prussia, along with the six other "perpetrators": Mrs. Molly Rush, director of the Thomas Merton Center in Pittsburgh; Sister Anne Montgomery of the Sisters of the Sacred Heart of Jesus, of New York City; Father Carl Kabat, O.M.I., a former missionary in the Philippines and Brazil; Elmer Maas, college professor and writer, New York City; Dean Hammer, a graduate of the Yale Divinity School, New Haven; and John Schuchardt, lawyer, father of three children, and member of the Jonah House community in Baltimore. Together they comprise what has come to be called the Ploughshare 8.

On arraignment, the court was not lenient. Dan and Phil Berrigan were held without bail, with bail for the others set at $125,000. It was a whopping amount by any calculation. A few days later, bail for the Berrigan brothers was also placed at $125,000. It was an amount that kept Phil effectively behind bars for months, as it did six others. Dan's bail was subsequently reduced to $50,000 because of health considerations. He had returned from the witness of Long Kesh with a severe viral infection, and once again prison authorities were not anxious to have on their hands a celebrity whose health was reason for their concern. The Jesuits came forth with bail for Dan, an astonishing development and one due chiefly to the influence of a new provincial. Never before had the order offered bail for Dan's release. It was a touching gesture, and one which seemed to accredit the observation made earlier by Dan, that at least there appeared to be more of a sense of value in the order for what he was about.

Federal authorities elected not to pursue charges against the Ploughshare 8, allegedly because they did not want to provide the defendants a public forum in which to articulate their views. The state, however, pressed ahead with its case. A magistrate dismissed five charges against the group, but left standing the counts of burglary, criminal trespass, criminal conspiracy, disorderly conduct, criminal mischief, simple assault, harassment, and criminal coercion. The trial approaches as this book goes to press.

One can guess what the outcome of the trial will be, and if not this one, then the next, or the next, or the next. It will be time behind bars.

Does this mean what Dan Berrigan and others like him are working against themselves and their cause by performing actions which put them in jails, where they are out of action, out of sight and, for many, out of mind? The case can be argued that some purposes are defeated or handicapped. On the other hand, there is the historical fact that, like the selfless person, like Christ himself, they did something so that others might be safe, be saved. It is no small claim to immortality.

In the context of the King of Prussia action, no one put it in better perspective than Father Francis X. Meehan of St. Charles Seminary in Overbrook, Pennsylvania. His words appeared on the Op-ed Page of the *Philadelphia Inquirer:*

"Like David they enter[ed] our industrial-military Goliaths not with grenades, not with dynamite, but with a carpenter's tool, a hammer, and that special tool of the Carpenter of Nazareth, blood offered for the life of the world.

"So they go to prison and they do it nonviolently. Their prison life becomes a priestly act, a liturgy putting their bodies where their words are. . . .

"So you ask, what are the Berrigans doing? They are trying to get through to our conscience. Our armaments of madness are a way of death, not life. Our God commands us to choose life!"

The comments amounts to a benediction.